An Insider's Guide to

Buying and Selling
Used Mobile
Homes

by Frank Rolfe
and Dave Reynolds

ISBN# 978-0-6151-8609-2

Contents

Introduction

If you have vacant lots in your mobile home park as most owners do today, you have two options. One is to do nothing and hope that mobile home dealers, or mobile home owners, will bring in a home to fill that lot in the normal course of business. The other is to proactively purchase mobile homes and bring them in yourself, with the intention of selling them or renting them. With the first option, you don't have a lot of control, except to do the best job you can in advertising the lots as available. In the second option, you will, in many ways, control your destiny. In a slow market, such as we are in right now, you need to be extra aggressive in filling up your lots if that is the goal. One way to accomplish this is to buy new and used homes to set the process in motion. You might be able to fill 2-3 lots per year waiting on dealers, or you could fill 12-24 a year buying them yourself.

Of course, there is a greater risk, time and effort in filling the lots yourself. Not only will your capital investment be huge, as there are virtually no lenders who will allow you to leverage your capital when buying mobile homes, but you will have an enormous time investment in procuring homes, moving and setup, remodeling homes, selling or renting homes, and the regular upkeep of same. It is a path that if you decide you want to go down, takes supreme dedication and steel nerve – once you begin, it is hard to turn back. You will have to morph your entire management structure to accommodate the additional duties of remodeling and servicing these rental or homes sold on notes.

Before you begin such an undertaking, it is essential that you fully understand all of the issues related to this concept, as well as to understand the nuts and bolts of how to buy and evaluate homes, as well as how to advertise and sell or rent them. That is the purpose of this section of the book – to explain all of the issues so you can make an educated decision to go forward or not, and then, if you decide to go forward, show you exactly how to do it the right way.

As an aside, there are many books that will tell you the wrong way to proceed. They leave out many important, and expensive, steps to convince you that this is a "get rich quick scheme". We have not left anything out. You will find that our advice is significantly different from everyone else's, and is based on our collective experience of owning and operating over $100,000,000 of mobile home parks and homes. We don't believe that our competitors can make that claim. And we don't think you will profit from their materials. You might even lose all of your investments.

If you ever have any questions on any of this material, we welcome you to contact us at the site www.mobilehomeparkstore.com and www.mhbay.com, the nation's leading sources of information on the mobile home and park industry.

Frank Rolfe & Dave Reynolds

The Winning Approach and Why Most Books are Wrong

There's no money in owning and re-selling or renting mobile homes. There, I've said it.

Anyone who tells you otherwise is wrong. That being said, <u>there's huge profit in owning and re-selling and renting mobile homes in your mobile home park as far as the increase in the value of your mobile home park property</u>.

That is the primary difference in our opinion on this process as compared to just about everyone else. We believe that only someone who owns the mobile home park makes money in selling and renting mobile homes, and even then, only in the increased value of the mobile home park. If you are buying, selling, or renting mobile homes in other people's mobile home parks, we believe that you are not creating any value with your time, effort and risk. We have tried it, and although we have had a couple of winner deals, the loser deals far outweigh the winners.

Let's examine this in more detail.

Selling Or Renting Homes In Other People's Parks

The Economics of Mobile Home Selling or Renting if You Don't Own the Mobile Home Park

Let's assume you don't own the mobile home park where the home is going to go. Here is what the economics look like for renting a mobile home:

COST OF MOBILE HOME INCLUDING FULL REFURBISHMENT, BLOCKING, LEVELING, SKIRTING, STAIRS AND A/C HOOK-UP:	$12,000
LOT RENT IN MOBILE HOME PARK:	$200 per month
RENTAL RATE FOR HOME:	$500 per month
INSURANCE COST:	$50 per month
PROPERTY TAX:	$30 per month
REPAIR AND MAINTENCE: (yes it's really that high)	$100 per month

SALES EXPENSE: lets assume you do it all yourself so $0

Sample Profit and Loss Statement

Revenue	$500 per month

COSTS

Lot rent	$200 per month
Insurance	$50
Property tax	$30
Repair and maint.	$100
Net income	$120 per month

Hey, that's only about a 10% return on investment!

But wait...it gets worse.

We've left out a few other real world expenses that need to be in there.

- Vacancy
- Bad Debt
- Evictions & Filing Fees
- Make-ready when the tenant destroys the house and steals all of the appliances.

When you add these items in, you are losing probably $100 per month, or more. Is this worth investing your time and money in if you <u>don't</u> own the park? Hardly.

The Economics of Selling and Carrying a Note on a Mobile Home That is in a Mobile Home Park You Don't Own

Okay, you agree that renting a mobile home is a money losing proposition. So what about selling the home and carrying a note on it? Well, sorry to say that it's a loser too.

COST OF HOME:	$12,000
LOT RENT IN PARK:	$200 per month
PRICE YOU SELL HOME:	$16,000 with $1,000 down and 12% Int
TOTAL MONTHLY PAYMENTS:	$200 Lot Rent + $250 Home Payment

Sample Profit and Loss Statement

Revenue	$450 per month
COST	
Lot rent	$200 per month
Net income	$250 per month

Before you get too excited, we have to make one big adjustment – that $250 is not going to last forever, in this case only for under 8 years – or 92 months (that's how long it takes to pay the house off). You have not created a lifetime of income, only for 92 months. And that's assuming the buyer makes the payments.

Have you heard about the sub prime credit mess? Well, guess what kind of customer you will be selling to? The lowest end of the credit spectrum – that's who. Based on national averages, even if you do all the credit screening in the world, they will stop paying you in the first two to four years. So you may be getting that house back when they default and run off (in our experience you get about 5 out of 10 homes back). What happens then? Well, first, you will have to file for a legal foreclosure, a much more expensive step than a simple eviction. And you will have to pay the lot rent during the entire process. But the worst surprise is that you will have to make the home ready to sell again. And wait until you see what condition it will be in! It's a pretty safe bet that the carpet will be stained and filled with pet urine. The walls will have holes and scrapes all over the place. The closet doors will all be broken. And the appliances (including A/C and heat) may be missing, being sold by the home owner to pay for their move.

To get that home back into service again will cost maybe $5,000 – and there goes any profit you thought you made. In addition, now the home is a few years older, and will not sell for as high a price as it did last time. And if this cycle repeats itself just one more time, you will be lucky to get for the home what you just spent in re-doing it.

Why do the other guys leave this important item out of their books? I approached one of them at a convention and asked him and his response was "I've never had to spend a penny on repairs on my houses". Then he must not have ever owned one!

Selling And Renting Mobile Homes In Your Park

The Winning Approach to Mobile Homes Sales and Renting

Here's the secret to making money. <u>You must own the park.</u> If you had owned the park in these two earlier examples, you received $200 per month in lot rent no matter what happened. Here's what that means to you as the park owner:

Sample Profit and Loss Statement

Revenue	$200 per month
COST	
Assume tenant pays all utilities	$50 per month
Net income	$150 per month

If you own real estate, you are probably familiar with the concept of a "cap rate" or capitalization rate. This is the number that correlates income to value of the mobile home park. Suppose that the cap rate on this park is 10%. Then here's where the big money is:

Net income:	$1,800 per year
Value at 10%:	$18,000

Under this scenario that old mobile home you just got on your vacant lot has made you $18,000 in value. Now <u>that</u> is where the money is.

As long as the sole focus on bringing in mobile homes to re-sell or rent is on the <u>financial impact to your mobile home park value</u>, then you are using the winning approach. But beware, because even using this approach, you still have to be careful of how much money you put into each house you bring in.

How To Calculate The Correct Price Range Of Homes To Bring Into Your Park

If you have calculated the value of each occupied lot to your overall park value, using a cap rate of about 10%, you know what the value is of each lot once you bring in a home. However, to make a profit you must spend considerably less than that amount on the homes you bring in.

In our earlier example, we learned that each occupied lot is worth an additional $18,000.

Under that scenario, we must spend less than $18,000 in money to fill that lot, or we accomplished nothing. So if we buy a mobile home including all costs and give it away for FREE, we are going to be ahead as long as we do not spend more than $18,000 on the home.

If we are going to buy a home for $25,000, we need to sell it for at least $7,000 after all costs to break even.

This is a very important point. The total you can spend is demonstrated in the following formula:

(Extra Value Created From Filling a Lot + Amount Collected From the Sale of Home) must be greater than (Cost of Home + Costs of Preparing Home For Sale + Costs to Foreclose + Costs to Make Home Ready to Sell Again)

In Dave's experience, taking all of the homes he has purchased and sold which is in the hundreds of homes, he has received about 60 cents on the dollar on the Purchase Price plus Cost to Move Home

In and Get Ready for First Sale. In Frank's experience, it is lower and approximates about 40 cents on the dollar on average.

So, lets take a couple of examples:

Extra Value Created By Filling a Space = $18,000

Cost of Home = $10,000

Cost to Move Home in and Setup for First Sale = $3,000

Amount Dave will Receive Based on His Experience = $13,000 x .6 = $7,800.

$18,000 + $7,800 = $25,800

So, in this case, $25,800 must be > $10,000 + 3,000 + Cost of Any Foreclosures + Cost of Making the Home Ready to Sell Again.

A more conservative approach is to value the mobile home at $0.

Now some people will tell you that we are crazy valuing mobile homes at $0.

However, we will tell you from over a decade of experience and hundreds of homes under our belt, that this may be exactly the case. Here's why. Mobile homes are constantly depreciating and falling apart. Every time you get one back, either through the end of a lease or default, or upon foreclosure, it's a wreck and can't be re-sold or re-rented until it has been fully rehabbed. At some point in its life, normally fairly early on, this "rehab" cost is more than the value of the mobile home. In addition, you will only get a fraction of the "rehab" cost up-front, so you only pocket less than the actual cost to fix it up. As a result, a home that churns tenants, which they can do, will actually cost you money in the long run. If you believe in the concept of income properties, you will quickly see that a business, in this case a mobile home that loses money every month is worth a negative number, but we are being charitable and call it $0.

I know it sounds crazy, but if you sell a used mobile home for $1, you may be better off than selling it for $20,000 and carrying paper on it. Why? Because at $1 the tenant will not need to be foreclosed on and should be able to pay the space rent. You may even be able to increase the space rent on this lot to increase the lot value even more.

Going back to our example, if you create $18,000 of value when you bring in a home that pays lot rent in your park, then you need to keep the cost of that home significantly under $18,000 if you want to make it worth the effort. You should try and hit a price of maybe $8,000 to $12,000 all bills paid. There is no right or wrong answer as to what the target profit should be. It is based on your desires and goals.

Once you have determined the value of each occupied lot in your park, then you can make a determination as to what the maximum price of a home to bring in to your park should be.

How to Find Homes in Your Price Range

Once you have determined your budget, you will need to find homes that fit into it. Many of you will find your budget to be pretty small. So here are some ideas of how to find houses to fit any budget.

But first, let's refine how much house we can buy, based on the other costs associated with moving a home into a park.

The costs of moving a home into a park include the following in addition to the home itself:

- The cost of hauling the home to the park, setting up, tying down, and leveling can cost about $2,000.

- The cost of skirting the home with new vinyl skirting is at least $500

- The cost of front and back stairs is about $500.

- The utility hook-ups (water, sewer, gas, and electric) are about $1,000.

So right off the bat, you have a fixed cost of $4,000 for the mobile home, without adding the cost of the home and refurbishment. If you ran the numbers on your park, and found that you have a budget of $10,000 per mobile home, then that means you really have a budget of only $6,000. So where do you find a home that's cheap? Here are some ideas for every price range.

$5,000 and under (which equates to a home of $1,000 or less)

Is it possible to find a mobile home that you can bring into your park, including refurbishment, for $1,000 or less? Yes, but it takes a lot of shopping. You will be looking for a home that is underappreciated, and one that you yourself can re-hab, so the problems have to be fairly cosmetic (or you have to be really handy). Where do you find a home like that?

- The backs of dealer lots. That's where the mobile home dealers put their trade-ins and repos that are too messed up to sell on the regular lot. You will be looking for beat up cosmetically, but good shape structurally mobile homes. And yes, they do sell them for $1,000 or less.

- Websites with Mobile Homes Listed for Sale such as MH-Bay.com and other home listing sites.

- Thrifty Nickel and other local newspapers – many of these also have the listings on line that you can sort through.

- Estate sales in mobile home parks. The heirs normally don't want to pay lot rent and don't want the mobile home. I've bought them for $1,000 before, and the condition was not bad.

- Inside your own park. You shave off the $4,000 of transport and set up, and you can increase your offer to $5,000 or less. If there is a risk that a home for sale will be pulled out of the park, it's a lot cheaper than bringing in a new one.

- Steal homes from neighboring parks. Offer the person a free move and set-up (cost $5,000 or less) and saves you from being in the middle of home ownership. One of the best promotions I have used in getting people to bring their home over from a neighboring park was to have a fully furnished unit in my park to allow these new residents a place to stay while their home is being moved and setup in your park. Like a motel but with all the conveniences of home.

$5,000 to $10,000 (which equates to a home of $1,000 to $6,000)

These homes are going to be the bulk of what meets your budget, unless you have a park with a higher lot rent, and want to make a decent profit on the lot value minus home cost formula. You can find these homes in the same place as the $5,000 and under, with a couple extra sources:

- Mobile home brokers. These are the guys that deal in repos from banks and other homes that have come to market from other distressed sources. They often have homes in the $5,000 range, and some are not bad.

- For sale by owner homes in other area mobile home parks.

$10,000 to $20,000 (which equates to a home of $6,000 to $14,000)

Now you are in the big leagues. I am guessing that you have a lot rent in your park of about $200 or more. If not you better check your math.

You have many, many more home options in this price range. Everyone, from dealer back-lots to brokers, will have homes to show you. In this price range, even dealer's main front lots may have some repos or trade-in options. In addition, there is one new source that has not been addressed:

- Mobile home manufacturers may have some <u>new</u> options for you to consider. Manufacturer's got so good at building cheap FEMA homes after Katrina, that they have some new models in this price range. Bear in mind that new homes don't require renovation, and sell or rent faster and for more money. You may be able to even get some <u>leverage</u> on your money (bank debt) for new homes.

$20,000 and above (homes from $16,000 and up)

In this price range, the world is your oyster, and you have an endless number of options. You may even look at some doublewides to spruce up key lots in your park. One word of warning, however, doublewides cost almost double that of singlewides to set up and tie down, as well as to move. The only thing that does not go up is the stairs. You need to factor in this greater expense before you run your numbers.

Now that you have your shopping list and budget, it's time to start looking at homes. The next section of the book is designed to do just that, and every home you look at should be based on the enclosed worksheet to make sure you don't make any errors.

Deciding Whether To Rent or Sell Mobile Homes You Bring In

Selling mobile homes and carrying paper, and renting mobile homes are two different business models. You need to give careful thought, before you begin, as to which one is more suitable for your goals and temperaments. Let's explore the differences in these two business models.

Selling and Carrying paper on Mobile Homes

In this function, you bring in a mobile home, sell it, and carry a note on it. You then service the paper like a bank. If you are very lucky, in some cases you may be able to sell a home for cash, but this is a fairly rare occurrence. Your target market does not have a lot of cash or credit, so it is normally impossible for them to come up with more than $1,000 or so as down payment.

The benefits of selling and carrying paper are numerous over renting.

- You do not have to perform repair and maintenance on the mobile home.

- You will attract a better quality customer, who will become an instant homeowner, and hopefully show pride of ownership.

- You will only have to show and sell (if you are very lucky) the home one time. And that also means only one make-ready.

- It is much more favorable to a bank or future purchaser that you have an owner-occupant and not a rental in your park. Some lenders will not allow you to have more than a few park-owned rentals in a park.

- It takes a whole lot less management to sell homes and carry paper than to rent them if you are an out-of state owner, or a passive investor. In this case this option is much more acceptable.

For most operators, selling mobile homes is the better and more profitable option over renting.

Renting Mobile Homes

Renting mobile homes is an extremely time and effort intensive business model, and is normally an unprofitable venture. Contrary to what you may read from other authors, nobody ever made much money renting homes. We cannot recommend you rent over sell, unless you are faced with some of the following issues:

- You cannot get a dealers license. In most states, you must have a dealer license to sell more than one home per year. If you cannot get a license, for some reason, then your only option is to rent. If you illegally sell mobile homes, then you face severe penalties. There are normally no such licensing issues to rent mobile homes.

- You are unable to sell mobile homes, because the demand is just not there. This doesn't happen very often, but if your park is in a declining area or the homes are old and run-down, people may not have an interest in buying, but may still rent at the right price.

- You plan to shut down the park at some point in the future and it is easier to rent and then non-renew leases than to require a home to be moved.

- You just want to be a rental landlord, and look forward to making continuous repairs as a hobby.

- You have a very small park, and need to stick with rentals to make the critical mass large enough to attract future buyers.

- If you do not fall into one of these categories, then renting is much less desirable a business option than selling.

How To Sell A Mobile Home

Before you meet with that first customer, there is a lot of advance work and preparation you must complete.

In reality, we are not ever going to sell a decent home for one dollar or just give it away. If you want to cut down on foreclosures and re-hab costs the key is to sell the home at a fair price with good terms. We have all heard the old adage that all your buyer cares about is the monthly payment. This may be true in the beginning but as time goes on and they begin to realize that the home is depreciating and they owe more than it is worth, their desire to fulfill the contract is weakened. When we have sold homes for what they are really worth and not what they are worth plus $5,000, the follow through by the buyer can approach 75% or more. Interest rates in the 8-10% range and 3-5 year repayment terms have worked the best.

Assuming you have bought, brought in, set-up and made ready to sell the mobile home, there are still more decisions to be made:

- What will the asking price, and minimum selling price be? It is impossible to go "up" with the price, so be sure to ask what you really want from the start. If your goal is to sell it for $15,000 then don't start off timidly at $14,995. You <u>never</u> get your asking price when you sell a house – leave yourself plenty of room to negotiate. The general rule of thumb is to ask 10% to 20% more than you hope to achieve. You will also need to set an absolute bottom price. If you do not have such a "rock bottom" price, then you will gradually drift down to near nothing with someone that is a hard negotiator. You have to be ready to say to the buyer "this is a great price and I won't go a penny lower. It's already a bargain".

- How much down payment will I require? The general rule is about $500 to $1,000. That's about all the normal buyer has available. If you can get over $1,000 or $2,000 that's great – but you better be ready to go lower or you may never sell anything. *In our experience, the best down payments are available when people are getting their income tax refunds.*

- What interest rate will I require on my loan? Before you decide, find out what the maximum amount is allowed by law. Be careful not to exceed this amount or you may be guilty of usury.

- How long will I set my amortization period at? This is the length of time to repay the loan. In general, the shorter the period, the less chance of default. Shoot for 5 to 7 years and try to avoid longer periods such as 15 or 30 years. The sub prime lenders have already scientifically proven that long amortizations don't work.

While you are deciding these options, you will also need to become an expert at the laws on selling mobile homes in your state. The first step is to become a licensed dealer. In most states, this means going to a class and getting a certain bond. Some states require tests and others don't. If you're required to be a licensed dealer in your state, then find out immediately when the next classes are and sign up. They don't hold licensing classes all the time.

In addition to becoming a dealer, you will need to construct a sale contract and make sure that it meets all the laws as well. You may need to have an attorney read it to make sure.

Finally, you need to obtain comps of what other parks are doing with their park-owned homes; how much, what interest rate, etc. You can normally accomplish this though "mystery shopping".

Once you have completed this step, you need to have a stack of credit applications and sales contracts at the ready, along with park rules and lot leases. You will probably get a lot of calls and lookers, and you want to be ready to start closing deals on day one. You will also need to become a master of the titling process and how to amend the title to show you as the lender.

The final step is to have some training on showing homes and meeting objections. You need to develop a standard process from incoming call, to showing, to filling out paperwork, to the move in. If you are an owner / operator, at least you don't have to retrain anyone. If you are relying on a staff, then you need to put together an Operations Manual for selling homes. There is no point in advertising the homes for sale if you have no system to process buyers.

Once you have this accomplished, it is time to advertise the home for sale. There are many different things you can try, and you should try them all at once to give yourself the best chance for a quick sale:

- Put an ad in the local newspaper under both the "mobile homes for rent" and the "mobile homes for sale" section. The ad should read "_____ bedrooms. $____ per month.

(___) ____-_____". An ad like that in most markets will bring in about 10 people per day.

- Put a prominent "home for sale" sign, with your cell phone number on it, in the yard of the mobile home, as well as at your entry, and in the window of the mobile home itself. You can find these at Home Depot or Lowe's.

- Put up flyers with "tear off" phone numbers at the bottom in Grocery Stores, Laundromats, and other places your potential tenants will visit.

- Offer referral fees to current residents.

- Contact the local dealers and tell them what you have – they might just send you someone who does not qualify under their programs.

You will need to develop great skill at showing homes to customers. They are not expecting too much professionalism in a mobile home park anyway, but you want to maintain as high a closing ratio as you can. A closing ratio is the equation of the number of showings divided by the number of closings.

There are certain steps you can take to maintain a higher closing ratio:

- Do not let anyone show a house that has no people skills. You either have them or you don't. If someone is hard pressed to say "hello" to other humans, then sales is not their forte. Find someone else.

- Make the home cosmetically pleasing. A lot of what makes the home look good is cheap to accomplish, like touching up paint and planting some flowers. Just because it is in a trailer park does not mean the people have zero aesthetic sensibilities.

- Make sure that the home is clean and smells clean. There is no bigger turn off to a buyer than filthy kitchens or bathrooms, or carpet that reeks of pet urine.

- Have your documents (contract, credit application, etc.) ready to sign up right now. Don't make the customer come back later. Think of the old adage "be easy to buy from".

How to Rent a Mobile Home

Renting mobile homes is much easier than the selling function on the front end, and much worse servicing on the back end.

All you have to decide up front is the rental amount you will seek and whether or not you will provide appliances. Other than that, you are in business. In addition you do not need to obtain any type of dealer's license. And the documentation you need to prepare is much less; sales contract, lot lease, bill or sale, etc. vs. a rental agreement.

The advertising for renting mobile homes is exactly the same as described in the selling section above. And, just like selling the home, in most markets your phone will ring off the hook.

The thing, as a rental landlord, you must become a master of all the laws regarding rentals in your city and state. There are normally minimum standards you have to meet, and also requirements on how fast you have to repair broken items.

The typical rental arrangement requires a deposit. You may have trouble getting more than about $200. Remember that you are typically renting to those with little money, bad credit, and no other choices available.

You may want to consider having your rent paid every two weeks, or even weekly, as opposed to monthly. It allows you to keep tabs on the tenant more consistently, and doesn't allow them to get as far behind in the rent before you take action. It also removes them from having to remember to save up for the rent out of their weekly checks (you hope they're employed).

The big challenge in renting mobile homes is handling the perpetual repair and maintenance issues and damage to the property caused by tenants that tear things up or leave in the middle of the night.

First some ideas on making the repairs more survivable:

- Have a repair phone number set up that goes to voice mail so you never have to hear it ring. You will retrieve these messages several times a day. If you give them your cell number, it will ring 24 hours a day and drive you insane. Rental mobile home tenants may call you at 3:00 am, drunk, to tell you that their door knob doesn't work. Or at 6:00 am on Sunday morning. Or on Christmas day. To maintain sanity in your life, don't let them ever reach you direct.

- Sort the repair issues that are phoned in into different "stacks" based on urgency. On the non-emergency stuff, like complaints on paint colors, let a day or so lapse before you call the customer back. That sends a message that you are not giving them "Ritz Carlton concierge" service in a trailer park.

- Know yourself what must be fixed under what time constraints as required by law. Don't let tenants railroad you into making stupid quick decisions by threatening to sue you or turn you into the city. Let them know that you know the laws, and don't care in the least about their threats.

- Remove most of the items that cause repair calls in a mobile home. For example, get rid of closet doors (especially sliding ones), replace plastic door knobs with metal ones, and remove window screens. Only provide what is required by law.

In addition, you need to minimize the cost of repairs for the enormous damage tenants create (either accidentally or on-purpose) which you discover when the tenant runs off.

- Remove all appliances and make them get their own. If they get them at a rent-to-own center, then you are no longer responsible for repairs. Plus, they cannot hurt you by stealing them.

- Replace central air conditioning and heating systems with window heat and air, if the home's electrical system allows for it. These cost a fraction of the central units.

- Replace carpet and pad with carpet and no pad or with vinyl flooring to alleviate carpet cleaning and pet urine issues.

- Use the same paint color on all units, so there is never any issue with matching paint.

- Make sure outside air units are secured beyond just sitting in the ground – bolt them down. They are way too easy for tenants to run off with and pawn.

Perhaps the difference between making money (or at least breaking even) and losing money in renting is how well you handle repairs and vandalism. That is where to put your concentration and efforts. In most markets, a chimpanzee can rent units all day due to high demand.

Conclusion

If you want to show significant occupancy increases in mobile home parks today, bringing in homes yourself is becoming mandatory. With dealers sales so low, the velocity you can fill lots is anemic. Decade long fill estimates are not acceptable for most operators. The only option open is to bring in homes yourself and rent or sell them.

Our current chattel crisis has happened before in the industry, and most of the survivors from that period brought in homes. That is why there are often so many park-owned homes that come with parks you buy today.

If you make the decision to bring in homes, it is essential that you do it in the only profitable way – to base your thinking on enhancing the value of your park and not making money on the homes themselves.

Very few people ever made money renting or selling mobile homes – they made it on increasing the value of their park by bringing in newly occupied lots.

If you must bring in homes, except in select instances, you are normally better off to sell and carry paper than to rent. Renting is very exhausting in many ways – financially, maintenance, and management – and can ruin the reason you got in the mobile home park business, which was to get out of the management nightmares of apartments or other multifamily.

It is a major commitment, from learning laws and finding homes, to the selling or renting process and servicing the rental or note. It is not to be taken lightly, or as a knee-jerk reaction.

We hope that if you follow the advice expressed in this book, and use the accompanying worksheets on each and every mobile home you look at, and stick to our financial formulas, you will make money in this risky but often necessary business model. If you have any problems, you can always reach us at www.mobilehomeparkstore. com.

Good luck, and hope to hear of your successes!

Frank Rolfe and Dave Reynolds

Book Number 2 - Forward

Buying a repo or used mobile home is an adventure with all the Hollywood theatrics of a movie – sad moments, happy moments, a cliff-hanger, and even a chase scene to hunt down the workman that never showed up as promised. The goal of this book is to make your movie have a happy ending, instead of one like a "Nightmare on Elm Street".

A used mobile home is the sum of many parts. While we have put down on paper every part of a mobile home in excruciating detail, it is up to you to add up these equations and decide whether or not the home is a good deal for you.

Read this book, think about the key issues, and enjoy your adventure!

Frank and Dave

How to Use This Book

This book is more than a book. It is a scorecard for the homes you are looking at buying. It is designed to be used as a scorecard, with every part of the home having its own line item.

You will find a worksheet at the end of the book that you should Xerox off and use a fresh sheet for every home that you are looking at buying. This will help make your decision to buy or not to buy more scientific and precise.

How To Find A Used Mobile Home to Buy

There are many different places to look for used mobile homes. As with anything, you will have your greatest success in volume, so you should work all of these angles at the same time to have the greatest number of candidates to choose from.

Websites

You can find thousands of mobile homes for sale immediately on MHBay.com, MHVillage.com, MobileHome.com and Mobile-Home.net. These listings often show photographs and other pertinent information, along with an asking price and phone number.

Dealers

Most mobile home dealerships have used homes on their lots. The nicer, pricier ones are at the front of the dealership, but there is another set at the back in a field that are the junky trade-ins they have collected along the way. These homes are normally older and in poor repair, but often make great homes to bring into a park or raw land if your goal is spend as little as you can. These homes are often sold for less than $1,000, sometimes for as little as $100, but they need total restoration. If you read this book, and look at enough candidates, you may find a diamond in the rough. Be sure to look past the cosmetic issues for the real meat and potatoes of what it will cost to restore.

Important: Be sure to know the laws or the city/state you are bringing the home into to make sure it is allowed. Some cities may require certain sizes or ages of homes. You don't want to buy a home and then not have a place to put it.

You can find a list of mobile home dealers by state on MHBay.com or MobileHomeParkStore.com.

Brokers

These individuals range from owners of 100 used mobile homes to as little as two or three. They act as a middleman between the used and repossessed homes found at dealers, banks and mobile home parks, and the buyer. You can find them sometimes in the newspaper, yellow pages, word-of-mouth, MobileHomeParkStore.com, or Google them. They serve a useful purpose because simply by moving the home from where it sits to their yard (if they have one) they demonstrate that it is road worthy. Of course, you may get a better deal without using a middleman, but not always. These middlemen buy in bulk and can often pass some of the savings on to you. We like to use reputable brokers because the time saved is worth the wasted time driving around and looking for homes.

Mobile Home Parks

At any given moment, there are probably one or two used mobile homes for sale in every mobile home park. You can find them by driving around and looking for home for sale signs in windows or yards.

Often the sellers of these homes want very little for them, particularly if they are moving and don't want to pay another month of lot rent. Also, often the seller is an estate and wants to sell it quick. **A big advantage of buying a home that is already set up in a park is the ability to test the electrical and water systems, as well as the AC and furnace.**

In Your Own Park (If Applicable)

If you own a mobile home park, don't forget to look inside your own park. While you are busy looking for homes to buy and bring in, don't let your existing homes move out if you can help it. If you do, you'll have to buy another to fill that spot. Often, when a home is already in your park, you are the most logical buyer since you don't have to pay to move it. This gives you the best pricing advantage. Remember, it cost thousands to move and set up a mobile home, so save this money on the front end by buying a used home for sale in your own park.

Newspaper

You will often find several mobile homes for sale in your local paper. These are often great prospects. Be sure to look not only in the big local paper, but also the thrifty nickel, penny saver, and other free papers that cater to the local markets. Also, it may be easier to visit these newspaper websites rather than build an office full of old papers. Check this site: americanclassifieds.com.

Place a Mobile Home Wanted Ad

You can post an ad in your own local newspaper or other publication stating that you are looking to buy a mobile home or homes. A simple 2 or 3 line ad in the paper may get your phone ringing. Another place to post an ad would be on the MobileHomeParkStore.com site under Investors Looking for Homes. This is a free listing and just another outlet to help you in your search.

Mobile Home Movers

Movers of mobile homes are often familiar with your market and know most of the parks and areas with a large concentration of mobile homes. Just like contacting a dealer and seeing what they have for sale on the back lot, stay in contact with the movers because they run across homes every day. Good movers are a great source of information and I have purchased many a home from a couple of the movers I know.

Financial Institutions

One of the easiest ways to find a repossessed mobile home is to contact the Mobile Home Lender and ask to be put on their mailing list. It is quick, easy and cuts out the middleman. With all of the foreclosures taking place, many finance companies have split their "Repo List Keepers" up into different areas so it may take a few calls or emails to find the right list to be on. However once you are on it, you will receive a list of fresh repossessed mobile homes to bid on, one or more times a month. Here is a list of Financial Institutions that have plenty of repos to go around, to help you get started.

Vanderbilt 865-380-3523 www.vmfrepos.com
Greentree 800-643-0202 www.gtservicing.com
Origen Financial 800-492-1874 www.ofllc.com
21st Mortgage 800-955-0021 www.21stMortgage.com
Triad Financial 904-223-1111 www.triadfs.com
US Bank 858-720-7116
Popular Housing Services 724-873-3543
www.tammac.com
www.origenhomes.com
www.21strepos.com
www.vmfrepos.com
GREENTREE REPOS
Greentree 800-643-0202 www.gtservicing.com

ALABAMA 800-940-3581
ARIZONA 800-328-8214
ARKANSAS 800-576-1021
CALIFORNIA 800-365-0089
COLORADO 800-525-8799
FLORIDA 800-874-1159
GEORGIA 800-874-1159
IDAHO 800-392-4276
INDIANA 800-532-7768
MICHIGAN 800-444-1968
MINNESOTA 877-245-6267
MISSISSIPPI 800-874-0793
MISSOURI 800-392-4276
MONTANA 800-548-2632
NEVADA 800-365-0089
NEW HAMPSHIRE 800-992-1018
OHIO 800-686-6600
OKLAHOMA 800-333-4482
OREGON 800-562-2510
SOUTH CAROLINA 800-922-0010
TENNESSEE 800-234-7101
TEXAS 800-772-5361
TEXAS 800-292-7413
VIRGINIA 800-669-2178
VIRGINIA 800-234-7101
WASHINGTON 800-562-2510
WISCONSIN 877-245-6267
CHASE BANK REPOS
WESTERN U. S. 888-667-9133
EASTERN U. S. 800-225-6761

If you work these seven angles simultaneously, you will never have a shortage of homes to look at, and may find some real gems.

How to Make the Offer

The first rule in getting a good deal on a used mobile home is to look poor. This will set a first impression with the seller of how high he can go on the pricing.

Be sure to wear beat-up clothes and drive your worst car to the meeting. Don't go in with a blazer and driving a Mercedes. You are not trying to impress the seller, only get a cheap deal.

Always offer a ridiculously low number on the front end. Say "this home is in pretty poor condition, and needs a lot of work. I'd be afraid to pay more than $500 for it", even if the home is in great condition. Let the seller's response give you a clue as to the real price he'll take. You may be surprised at how little he'll take for the home. If you offer a big number on the front end, you can't lower it later. So be very prudent about what you offer.

Be sure and look thoroughly at the condition of the home using our spreadsheet. Make sure you've put all the correct numbers in for repairs.

If you have built a large enough base of homes to look at, you should not be all that emotionally tied to any home. If you truly aren't, the seller will feel that vibe and be more negotiable. And if the home looks like a bad deal, just say so and leave. Often, many of the problems will cost you so much that you should not take the home even for $1.

Paperwork And Looking For Other Deal Killers

When buying a used mobile home, there are many pitfalls that you must be aware of, and some basic contract issues that you need to do properly.

Bill of Sale

This is the document that confirms the exchange of the home from the seller to the buyer, and affirms the price. This document is often on just one side of an 8½" x 11" sheet of paper. It should be notarized and signed by both parties. It should reference the serial number of the home, the make and model, and the date of manufacture (if possible). It should also contain the full price and any other items that go with the home, such as outside A/C unit, decks, etc.

A sample Bill of Sale is attached at the end of this book.

Title

A Bill of sale is not enough to properly document the sale. You also will need to obtain, sign and properly file for a title transfer of the mobile home. The title is the paperwork that, in most states, defines who owns the home, as well as whether or not it has a lien.

Sometimes, the seller will not have a title. This is a big problem. Without the title, you may be buying a home with a lien on it – or perhaps that he doesn't even own. There have been many stories of a renter trying to sell the home he lives in but does not own – don't be a victim. If there is no title, you will also have trouble re-selling the home down the road. It's a business decision for you to make, but in general, I would not buy a home that has no title. The downside is just too great and it may be illegal in some states.

Liens

If you buy a home that has a title but shows a lien on it, you must get that lien off the title before you should buy it. In most states, the lien holder technically owns the home until their lien is paid off. It is not uncommon for a lender to come back on a new owner and demand their home back. In addition, there may be legal issues and penalties in such a situation. Don't let that situation occur to you. Only a title with no liens can give you that piece of mind.

We have all seen those ads in the paper for homes and cars for sale advertising to just take over payments. Unless you file the correct documentation with the actual lender, you will be in jeopardy of losing the home if the lender finds out it has been sold. I have seen many people do this in the past and have never heard a success story. The lender either calls the note or the seller collects the payment from the buyer and doesn't pay the lender. Don't get yourself in a situation such as this.

Property Taxes

If you buy a mobile home without checking first, and there are unpaid property taxes on it, they are now <u>your</u> responsibility to pay. That's why it is essential that you check with the local taxing authority on the mobile home you are considering buying to make sure that there are no unpaid property taxes.

In most states today, you have to show a document to evidence that there are no property taxes before you can get a moving permit. If there are taxes, there is no way to get around paying them and the taxes can be staggeringly high. I have seen $10,000 unpaid property tax bills. And it is very normal to have at least $2,000 in unpaid taxes. Don't let this happen to you.

Unpaid Lot Rent

If the mobile home is located in a mobile home park, and there is past due rent on it, the park owner is not obligated to let you remove it until the rent is paid. At $200.00 per month or more for lot rent, it is not hard for the rent to stack up rapidly. I have seen unpaid lot rent bills in the thousands. Be sure and check with the mobile home park <u>before</u> buying the home to make sure that there is not any unpaid lot rent charges owed. This may also be the case in some land/home communities.

Access to Home

If the mobile home is in a field or remote area, make sure that you have the access to remove the home. Sometimes, over the years, the access has gone away, through new trees growing or a bridge washing away. Make sure that you are buying a home that can be moved to where you want it.

I made this mistake once on a home near San Antonio, TX. I bought a nice 16' x 70' home from Greentree and sent the mover out to have it moved to my park. Once the mover was there, he called me and said that there was no way to get the home out without crossing the neighbor's yard. The home was on a hill and had to be pulled through a low area and would have bottomed out and been stuck. The neighbor was nice enough to let us pull it through his yard after about a month of negotiations. We ended up paying him $1,000.00 in cash plus about $750.00 to buy him a new fence that we had to pull down.

How To Transport

Once you've made your mobile home selection, the next challenge is getting it moved to your lot. Moving a mobile home is unlike any other transportation you've ever been involved in.

The term "mobile" in mobile home is a little misleading. There is nothing really mobile about this thing. And the home doesn't enjoy being moved any more than you do. Fortunately, once you get it in position, you hopefully won't have to ever do it again. But there is no greater sigh of relief than once it has been safely delivered.

Also, it is important to remember that the frame and axles are designed to move the home as it came from the factory. The extra weight of your furniture and other belongings may cause problems during the move. Also make sure that you take down any mirrors or other breakables as well as tape the drawers and cabinets closed and secure the appliances so they are not moving around while the home is in transit.

Finding a Mover

There are really three sources of names and numbers of movers and, like looking for a home; you should talk to all of them to see who has the best deal and timing.

The first source is your local yellow pages. Most larger metro areas have a section on Mobile Home Movers or Transporters. There will probably be three to five names in that section for you to call.

The second source is the internet. You can go to MHBay.com or you can Google up "mobile home movers in (your town)". Normally this may bring up one or two that were not in the yellow pages.

Finally, and most importantly, is calling all of the mobile home dealers and finding out who <u>they</u> use to move their mobile homes that they sell. Since they sell mostly new, expensive homes, this subset of movers are often the best.

It is not recommended to use Uncle "I Got Truck" Jack from down the lane. Doing so may end up costing you more than the home will ever be worth. Stick with reputable moving companies, and always make sure they have insurance to cover any mishaps that may occur while they are in possession of it.

Having the Mover Inspect the Home

This step is even better if you can have it done before you buy the home, in case there are any deal killers that you haven't noticed. The key issues are 1) is the frame O.K. 2) Can they get the tongue on it and is it safe. 3) Do they have the necessary wheels and axles and 4) can the mover actually get the home moved (access issues).

Only the mover can give you the price of performing these items and it is highly variable. While selecting the mover, you need to get the price in writing, as it can be very different from one mover to the next, and is mostly labor. I always try to get three competitive bids. This gives you the best chance for getting a good price.

The bid should include the tongue, adding wheels and axles and delivering it to the site. You should also discuss some what-if scenarios such as the frame breaking in transport, etc., so that you have some kind of fall-back plan in the event that something goes wrong.

It is also important when selecting a mover to make sure they are licensed and insured. You don't want to have some fly-by-night company moving your home down the road.

Have the Property Taxes Paid Well in Advance of the Move

In most states, you have to show proof of paid property taxes before the mobile home can be moved. So don't procrastinate getting this done in advance. This is a very common hold-up to getting the home moved, and there is no reason for it.

Hopefully, you checked on the taxes owed before you bought the home, so there are no unhappy surprises.

On the Day of the Move

Be sure to be on location at the site it is going to when it arrives, since you only get to move it once under most contracts. Once the moving truck is gone, you will have to pay to have them come back. Be sure that you know where the utility lines and connections are at the new location, as well as the required setbacks. Also make sure that you have obtained necessary city clearances or permits to bring the home in.

If the home arrives late, don't get bored and leave. It will probably arrive once you have left, and you will have no say-so over the position the mover leaves it in. Plan to devote an entire day to "being there".

Don't Pay Until the Job is Done

Never make the mistake of paying the mover in advance of the move. Once he is paid, the mover may not bother with your move until all of the other paying customers are over with. Only pay once the home has been delivered in an acceptable manner.

There are some movers out there that have been known to collect fees and never perform. If they require payment up front, look for the next mover. You could always use an escrow service in extreme circumstances.

How To Set And Tie Down

Once the home has been delivered, it is time to prepare to make it a "permanent fixture". This requires blocking it, setting it, leveling it, and tying it down.

Blocking It

Mobile homes, as you have probably seen already, are supported by halite blocks stacked underneath the frame. These blocks take all of the weight of the load. There are state laws on the correct ways to block a house and, while you may have no idea of what these are, do question it if you see one end of the home way up in the air (like on a hill) and if the blocks are not straight or perpendicular to the ground. If the home falls off the blocks you will have a disaster on your hands.

Leveling It

Once the mobile home is up on blocks, it must be leveled. Without this important step, the doors and windows will not function properly, and the floors will make you sea-sick. Leveling is not subjective – if you don't think the home seems level then say something. There are few things more disturbing to the potential buyer or tenant than a home that is not level.

Before hiring the person that is going to be setting up your home, make sure the person does have the necessary equipment to do the job right. Find out what tool they will be using to level the home. A hand-held framing level, a dump truck to move the home, and jacks meant for changing car tires should not be acceptable. These types of tools are a dead give-away that the person you are about to hire is an "Uncle Jack" from down the lane. Stay clear of them, they will only cost you more money and headaches.

Tying it Down

The final step in setting a home and making it ready for someone to live in it is tying the home down to the ground to give it strength against wind and hold it in position on its blocks. The biggest danger here, if you are using a licensed mobile home installer, is hitting a utility line with the 4 foot anchors – big metal screws that go about three feet into the earth. If they hit a water or sewer line you will have to patch or replace it, and if they hit a gas line or underground electric line, it could result in injury or death. Be sure to have a really good handle on where your utility lines are prior to this step.

Setting and tying down a mobile home requires a professional who is licensed and insured. There are many different ordinances regarding these steps, and you cannot possibly advise anyone of the correct way to do these things. So never offer your advice to a professional, and never even think about doing these things yourself. The liability, if you did so, could be enormous, and there are significant fines in most states as punishment for anyone who tries to perform these tasks themselves.

In many cases you will use the company that moved the home in to perform the setup process. As said before, make sure that whoever you hire is licensed and insured. When calling movers out of phone books or from directories such as those on MHBay.com and MobileHomeParkStore.com, always make sure of their qualifications. Many states have websites that you can check to see if the mover and installer are actually licensed.

A Quick Spotter's Guide To A Used Mobile Home

YOU CAN TELL A LOT ABOUT A MOBILE HOME WITH-
OUT GOING INSIDE

Roof Type and Date of Manufacture

You can get a rough idea of the age of a mobile home based on its roof design.

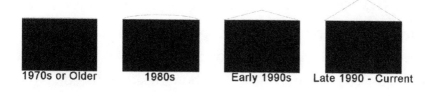

Size of Home

Mobile home "box" sizes are measured not including the tongue of the home. Be sure that you focus on the "boxes" size and not the overall size (which includes the tongue). The tongue is usually removed as part of the setup and skirting process.

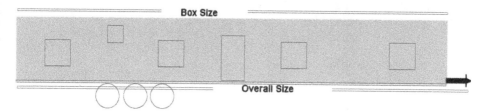

Roof Type

There are two roof types on a mobile home: 1) metal 2) shingle. Shingle is more expensive, and the better homes have shingle roofs. The difference, however, between metal and shingle is mostly aesthetic.

Siding Type

There are three types of siding on a mobile home (not counting the strange things that a tenant may have patched over with later). The three types are vinyl, metal, and "wooden".

Of these three types, the one to avoid is the "wooden" (it isn't real wood and it rots <u>very</u> easily).

Frame Integrity

For this home to be moved from point A to point B, it has to be road worthy. Unfortunately, many are not. If you buy a home that can't be moved, you may have just bought a liability that you will have to pay to get hauled to the dump, or torn down on location.

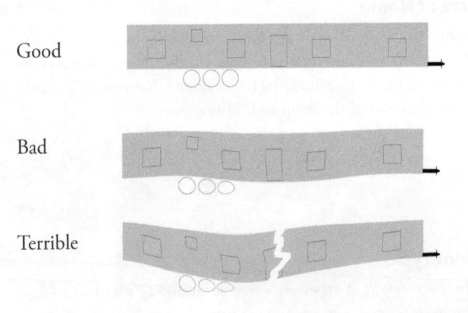

How To Sell Or Rent The Home

If you are buying the used mobile home for your own use, then you can disregard this section. If you follow and understand the other chapters, your job is done – congratulations! However, if you are not the end user, you have one final, important job to complete.

Before you rent or sell the mobile home, there are some important decisions you have to make. If you are thinking of selling the home, and will sell more than one home per year, you may have to get a Mobile Home Dealer's License. Check with your state to see what the requirements are. This step will require, in most states, going to dealer school, obtaining a bond and insurance, and other requirements. If you do not want to take this step, then your only option is to rent the home.

Another decision to make is how you feel about making repairs. The biggest difference between renting a mobile home and selling it… is when you rent it you are typically responsible for maintenance. If you do not want to do regular maintenance on the home, you will have to sell it and you may have to get that dealers license.

Once you have decided to either sell or rent, the next step is to come up with a rental or sales price. The key consideration in pricing is how much the market can afford to pay. In our opinion, the magic number in most parks is $500.00 per month in total payments. For example: If you want to sell the home, and the lot rent in your mobile home park is $200.00 per month, then you have about $300.00 per month to play with. Given you have $300.00 for a monthly payment you need to get out an amortization table and see what the price would be with $500.00 to $1,000.00 down and payments of $300 per month for between 5 and 7 years. That number will set your price. You will need to insert an interest rate in that calculation, say 10% and that choice is yours (be sure not to exceed usury laws).

If you are renting the home, then you can just pick a rental rate, and we would propose that the correct rate should not exceed $495 per month. But again, it is up to you to do some market research and if you can get more than $495 per month, then good for you.

Once you have decided what your price should be, the next step is to properly advertise it. We have tried a lot of different advertising options, and the following are the most effective in our opinion:

- The big local newspaper. Be sure to put your ad in both the "mobile homes for sale" and "mobile homes for rent" sections. You may also try putting the ad occasionally in Spanish to see if that pulls.

- Sign in the window or yard of the home saying "Home for Sale" or "Home for Rent". You can buy these at Lowe's or Home Depot. Be sure to put your phone number on it with a big, thick marks-a-lot, not a ballpoint pen.

- Tear sheet at local grocery stores and Laundromats (these are the sheets of paper with phone numbers that you rip off the bottom).

- Yellow page advertising. This is an option that only works if you intend to sell more than one home and are going to do this year round, since the ads are sold on a yearly basis only.

- You may also set up a commission only with local dealers that may have customers who do not qualify for standard bank loans, so that they can still make money on customers even if they turn them down for a new home.

- Giving $100.00 or more for referrals to people to send you a buyer can help also. Just make sure the referrer knows that they do not get paid unless their referral buys.

Some of the advertising options that do not work in our opinion:

- Greensheet, Thrifty Nickel or Penny Saver types of newspapers. We have tested these and there was virtually no response.

- Radio, TV or any other type of costly, structured advertising program.

Now that you have some people calling to see the home, the next step is organizing a program to effectively show the home. The first step is to make sure that the home is ready to sell or rent – all of the renovations should be complete. Most importantly, the home should have solid functioning stairs with a handrail. You would not believe how many slip and fall cases there have been for people looking at mobile homes without good stairs and falling down the stairs. Make sure that you have the home done with skirting in place and good stairs before you show it. If you are not done with your renovations, then hold off marketing the home until you are done.

The person who shows the home must have the right personality to make it a success. They need good people skills and a practiced sales pitch, just like a regular realtor. If the person showing the home does a poor job then, no matter how good you advertise it, it will not sell or rent. Feel free to mystery shop the person showing the home and see what their experience is. If your mobile home park manager is a lousy salesperson, you may want to enlist the help of someone else in the park that has sales experience, and pay them a commission if it sells or rents.

Let's say that you now have a customer who wants to buy or rent the home, so it is time to complete the screening and paperwork process. Credit and criminal screening is available for a nominal fee from many different vendors. You can find them by doing a simple search on your favorite search engine. The cost is about $10 to $30 per application. The problem with screening is that most of the applicants are going to have pretty poor credit and possible some non-violent criminal issues. So you have to decide what you are trying to achieve. If you are going to accept anyone who walks in the door, then there is little point to screening. Further, the most hardened criminals know ways around the screening process, such as knowing which states don't share criminal information, or having a friend or family member do the application process, and then pretend to go on vacation and have the real person move in.

The paperwork for renting or selling a mobile home is pretty easy and straightforward. It includes a sales contract, a copy of which is attached or, in the case of renting, a rental agreement (a sample is attached). Be sure to get a decent deposit (at least $500.00) and the first months rent or house payment in advance. If you get nothing down, then you risk having the person move in, pay no rent, trash the house, steal the fixtures, and have nothing to show for it. Often the deposit will not cover all the damage done by the tenant, but at least it gives you something to mitigate this expense, as well as prove to you that the customer has at least some money in his pocket.

Unfortunately the final item that you have to be familiar with is the eviction or foreclosure process. Even the best tenant sometimes turns bad, and so it is a pretty safe bet that at some point in the future you will need to file a motion to get your property back. Always think of everything that happens with your tenant as putting together a paper trail for a future court date. Keep all correspondence, postmarks of late payments, etc. in a file. When you have to file an eviction or foreclosure, this will all be important information to have going in to prove your case.

Dave and I both believe in the theory of "no pay/no stay". Everyone must pay their rent every month, or get out. There can be no exceptions. Start the eviction or foreclosure process immediately following the event of non-payment. Be sure to know the laws on the demand letters and other notifications that the court requires.

If you do not like going to court, you may hire a lawyer (there are normally landlord evictions attorneys at a lower price). Don't avoid starting the process for that reason. There is no reason not to start the eviction process immediately. It's always the right thing to do.

Five Worst Used Mobile Home Deals We Have Ever Done

1. This was a mobile home that I bought set up in a mobile home park that was being torn down. It looked great all blocked up but when they jacked it up to transport it to my park, it looked like a big smile, with a huge sag in the middle. I had to get it out anyway, so we took it out on the highway and it immediately proceeded to break in half. I then had to pay to have it taken to the dump and destroyed. My $1,000.00

investment cost me over $3,000.00 to get rid of. How's that for a bad return on investment?

2. This was a mobile home I bought for $500.00 at the back of a dealer's lot. I bought it because it was to fit a specific sized lot I had. The dealer told me the length, but I never went out and measured it myself. The dealer was wrong. The home was ten feet longer than the lot it was supposed to go on. It would not fit anywhere in the park and nobody would buy it from me. So I had to take it to the dump to be destroyed. Total return: $500.00 bought me a $3,000.00 loss.

3. This was a mobile home that I bought at the back of a dealer lot for about $500.00. The home was supposed to be all electric. Once again the dealer was wrong and I never checked into it. It was all gas. The park I had brought it to was all electric and the mobile home wasn't worth enough to convert to all electric. Off to the dump again!

4. This was a mobile home that I bought set up in a park. It looked good aesthetically. But it was a rust-bucket under all that paint and silk flowers. When we went to renovate it, everything was shot. We ended up tearing it down on location. $1,000.00 investment got me $2,000.00 in removal fees.

5. This was not a mobile home. This was an RV I bought to fill a really small lot (24' length), that I intended to rent out. Not only are RV's rotten rental properties, but the kind of tenant this one attracted made America's Most Wanted look like the I Love Lucy Show. I gave it away to a local RV dealer just to get rid of it. I got tired of all the police reports.

Five Best Mobile Home Deals We Ever Made

1. During the peak of the chattel crisis, there was a mobile home that was abandoned in our park with a mortgage company as the responsible party. They were supposed to get it out by a certain date, but when that day approached nothing had been done. I started bugging the account representative and he offered to sell me the home for $1,000.00. In effect, I had purchased a home with a $30,000.00 mortgage for only $1,000.00.

2. I purchased a group of 10 new homes from a factory to fill 10 short 48' lots I had in two different parks. The homes looked great and I sold them immediately for what I had spent on them. I got a better class of tenants due to their great condition and nobody ever defaulted when I sold them. They were relatively inexpensive as I had ordered them stripped of all the luxuries. They cost about $14,000.00 each installed.

3. I purchased a real Junker in a park and had it moved to our park. It was a pre-HUD (pre-1976 construction) – more like 1876. It had a flat roof and about as much modern appeal as an old Buick, but it was built incredibly well. Solid mahogany paneling and cabinetry. It even had a built in Murphy bed. This was a top of the line model back before cars were invented. It needed very little renovation, and was built so well that it never fell apart in between tenants.

4. This was an average home that needed some work, but the guys moving it into the park crashed it into a building. The

mover's insurance did a lot of the renovation for me at no cost, and kept my basis incredibly low.

5. I bought a home at a park that was closing down, and just by being there in the park several times, I convinced other tenants to move their homes to my park. By the time I was done, I had brought 6 more mobile homes with me at no additional cost of my own.

Mobile Home Buyer's Worksheet

	Type	Anticipated Cost	Notes
Purchase Price of Home			
Moving & Setup			
Tongue			
Wheels and axles			
Frame			
Roof			
Roof Flashing			
Insulation & Vapor Barrier			
Siding			
Skirting			
Stairs			
Decks			
Awning			
Carports			
Windows			
Screens			
Doors (exterior)			
Doors (interior)			
Doors (closet)			
Ceiling			
Floors			
Carpet			

	Type	Anticipated Cost	Notes
Pad			
Vinyl floor			
Walls (interior)			
Counters			
Kitchen			
Bathroom			
Utility			
Cabinets			
Kitchen			
Bathroom			
Utility			
Appliances			
Central A/C			
Window A/C			
Window Heat/Air			
Furnace			
Ducts			
Hot Water Heater			
Electrical Box			
Electric wiring			
Light fixtures			
Water lines			
Sewer lines			
Gas lines			
Tubs			
Toilets			
Sinks			
Kitchen			
Bathroom			
Fireplaces			
HUD seal			
Serial #			

Tongue

What Is This?

This is the "v" shaped metal piece on the front of the home that allows it to be pulled by a truck.

Types?

There are two types of tongues:

Welded on (permanent and not meant to be removed)

Bolted on (only installed when moving home, then taken off)

Benefits & Drawbacks To Each?

Welded on tongues are not very good looking once the home is delivered. They are always there to remind you that it is a mobile home. However, you can have the tongue removed even if welded on (it is just an added cost to remove it and then to weld it back on in case you need to move the home again).

Bolted on tongues allow you a more aesthetically pleasing end-product.

Both types of tongues have the same function and require the same engineering.

How To Check For Problems?

On welded-on tongues, look for any broken weld or rust that might suggest that the tongue cannot pull the home safely.

On bolted-on tongues, make sure it is there. Many a novice has bought a home with the assumption that the tongue is stashed under the skirting; only to find that it is missing. If the tongue is there look for rust or welding issues that would preclude transport.

How To Fix Those Problems?

If you are not a certified welder, I would not try to fix these problems. They require welding skills with a pretty tough liability if you do it wrong; the whole home will break free on the highway at 55 mph.

How Difficult To Fix?

Extremely. Always use a professional, insured, certified welder. The liability is huge. If the home breaks free at 55 mph, it could cause massive property damage and / or death.

Estimated Cost To Fix?

To re-weld a tongue on a home can run about $300.00 or more based on the problem. Be sure to get three competitive bids. If you buy a home with a bolted on tongue that is no longer there, you can usually rent them from the mover for an extra $150.00 or so.

Other Thoughts

Before you think the tongue is missing, have a good look around the yard (if it's still in a park). I have seen them where they should be (under the house) and I have seen them in many places they shouldn't be (inside sheds, used as edging in a flower bed, and just laying out in the weeds at the back of the lot).

Wheels & Axles

What Is This?

These are the things that enable the mobile home to move. They fit on the carriage of the mobile home and make it mobile.

Types?

There are a variety of wheel and axles combinations, but they do not need to be of interest to you. The only thing that is important is that they function and allow the home to be safely transported from point A to point B.

Benefits & Drawbacks To Each?

Does the home move safely or not? That's the only thing to worry about. Unless you are opening a wheel and axle museum, the type should be of no consequence to you. Only the mobile home mover cares.

Often, the mover will have to provide the wheels and axles. This will cost you additional money when moving the home.

On a really old home, perhaps pre-1976, it may be a challenge to find wheels and axles that will fit. Make sure that the mover has access to what you will need, or your home may be un-transportable.

How To Fix Those Problems?

Let the mover tell you what the problem/solution is. The worst case scenario, like a broken frame, is that the home can't be moved. Rarely, however, are the wheels and axles a real issue. But be sure to put this risk in your budget.

How Difficult To Fix?

Don't even think about it. If you screw up the wheels and axles and the home breaks loose or rolls over, the liability is enormous. Only let the professional handle securing the wheels and axles.

Estimated Cost To Fix?

A set of wheels and axles costs about $75.00 to $100.00 to rent for the day.

Other Thoughts

It is amazing to me that movers have wheels and axles to fit almost anything. Mobile homes have the crudest construction of anything short of a pinewood derby. Many movers will just slap something on and go. Be sure to negotiate up front with the mover on the price to rent the tongue.

Frame

What Is This?

This is the series of steel rails and "outriggers" that comprise the chassis of the mobile home. The whole home is built on top of this.

Types?

Essentially, there is only one type. It is two or more steel rails, which have the axles attached underneath, and the mobile home built on top. It is just like the chassis of a car.

Benefits & Drawbacks To Each?

A good frame will hold the mobile home up in a straight line parallel to the ground, and allow itself to be pulled with a truck when the wheels and axles are attached.

If a frame is not in good shape, the home will have a "sagging" appearance, and may not be able to be moved by a truck.

A weak frame has the further liability issue of breaking while going down the highway at 55 mph.

How To Check For Problems?

Visually, look for any sagging or bending in the home when it is up on its wheels and axles.

Unfortunately, many people buy mobile homes that are still up on cinderblocks and tied down, which masks these issues.

If a frame is weak, you have to see it up on its wheels and axles before you can tell. To avoid being ripped off, you may ask the seller to do this before paying for the home.

How To Fix Those Problems?

You pretty much can't afford to fix a home with a bad frame (just like a cheap car with a bad frame).

If a frame is bad, you may not be able to move the home or, even worse; it can break in half while going down the highway, which may cause major property damage and/or death. In addition you will have to spend thousands just to get it hauled off to the dump.

How Difficult To Fix?

So difficult that I won't waste your time even explaining how it might be done. Sometimes, in a pinch, a good mover can put a few rails under it to transport it to the dump, but even that is risky.

Estimated Cost To Fix?

A fortune. Don't even think about buying a mobile home with a bad frame. The cost of disposal alone is in the thousands.

Other Thoughts

There is no feeling worse than having a mobile home you just bought for $1,000.00 break in half out on the highway and now you have to spend $3,000.00 getting it hauled off and destroyed at the dump. Not to mention that you may be blocking traffic on the highway and running the risk of incredible liability the entire time. If you even think that the frame is bad on the home, then go to the next deal immediately and never look back.

Also, make sure that you have insurance on the home either through your insurance carrier or the mover's policy.

Roof

What Is This?

This is the part of the house whose job is to keep the water out when it rains or snows.

Types?

There are basically two types on a mobile Home:

1. metal - looks like strips of aluminum foil
2. shingles – similar to single family home roofs

Benefits & Drawbacks To Each?

Metal roofs comprise probably 70% of all roofs. They used to be the industry standard. They are a fairly simple design. As long as there are no holes in them, and they are coated with (often white) roof "tar", they are pretty much good to go. The main drawback to this type of roofing is that it has no strength from anything besides rain and snow. If you step on it you may fall through it or cause the joints to leak. To inspect it, you are better off using a ladder to look at it without stepping on it so you can avoid causing damage.

Shingle roofs have the same problems as regular single-family homes. All of the shingles must be on the roof and in good shape, and the decking that holds the roof should not have too much sagging. The benefit to the shingle roof, other than aesthetic, is that you can gingerly walk on it if you must. But try to avoid doing so.

How To Check For Problems?

Most roofing problems are better discovered inside rather than outside.

On the outside, look for holes, rust, and whether or not the roof has been "coated". Also look for any rot or discoloration on the outer walls of the house, which may be a sign of leaks.

On the inside, look for discoloration on ceilings or "soft spots" on walls and floors, as sign of leaks.

How To Fix Those Problems?

On metal roofs, you can patch the holes and put a new coating on them. On shingle roofs, you can replace shingles, or decking, just like a regular roof.

One product that you might want to use is called Peel and Seel. It comes in various widths and lengths and is easy to apply if you follow the directions. I have found it a better lasting product than the elastomeric coatings. The only problem is that it costs over a dollar per square foot so you may only want to use it as a patching solution rather than a complete new roof.

The elastomeric coatings that you can buy at your mobile home parts store or Home Depot are another solution. I have had varying degrees of success with this product. It does not last as long as the previous solution but it is cheaper.

Due to access (you can't put a lot of weight on the roof) it is fairly hard to make substantial repairs. You can, however, buy all the parts you need from a mobile home supply store, and it isn't rocket science to apply.

How Difficult To Fix

Due to access, it is fairly difficult to fix more than the "easy" things, such as re-coating the roof with sealer. You always need to put your weight on a ladder, rather than the roof, if you can. Like any roofing job, have a buddy nearby in case you fall.

Estimated Cost To Fix?

Sealer costs approximately $60.00 per 5 gallon bucket. A normal roof will require one or two buckets. Shingles and decking will require pricing out at a roofing supply store.

Other Thoughts

The first time you work on a mobile home that has a metal roof you need to understand where to step and where not to. It can be just like walking in an attic of a single family home. Step in the wrong place and you might fall through the roof. Walking on a metal roof can feel a lot like walking on the roof of a tent.

How many times have you seen a mobile home with 20 tires or more on the roof? The reason that they are up there is not for storage for the junk car in the yard. They are there because when the wind blows, the roof rattles like it is going to fall off. The tires supposedly stop this rattle. A better solution to this is to firm the roof up with things called rumble buttons. Basically these are just screws that go through a washer with a rubber backing and are fastened to the roof trusses. Make sure to cover the screws and washers up with some coating to keep them from leaking if they loosen up.

Roof Flashing

What Is This?

This is the metal strip that keeps the water from coming in between the roof and the walls, or the ventilation pipes in the roof and where they meet the roof.

Types?

All mobile home roof flashing is metal (thin gauge sheet metal). As important as the metal, however, is the gooey sealant that helps hold it all together.

Benefits & Drawbacks To Each?

There is no certain benefit or drawback to the flashing. But it is a very complicated thing to fix. We have had houses that failed in two or three attempts to correct the flashing. Despite repairs, the homes would still take on water when it rained. Before you begin to work on it, be sure to put a lot of thought and study into how it works.

How To Check For Problems?

Roof flashing issues will manifest themselves on the outside, in the form of rotted walls (particularly with "wooden" sided homes) and on the inside, with weak spots in floors near the walls, ceiling discoloration, and rotten wall areas.

Often, flashing problems will be mistaken for roof issues, as the signs of trouble are similar. Flashing problems are not nearly as easy to see from the outside.

How To Fix Those Problems?

You have to replace or modify the existing flashing in the area affected. This requires the correct parts, which can be readily bought beforehand from a mobile home part supplier.

How Difficult To Fix?

Extremely difficult if you are new to this. I have found that to get the job done right requires a professional in most cases. Regular handymen's jobs started leaking again after a short period of time (if not immediately). Also access is difficult (from a ladder), and you can fall off and hurt yourself.

Estimated Cost To Fix?

To replace, or fix, the flashing on a roof of a 76' home (by a professional) will run you somewhere in the $300.00 range. The parts are relatively cheap, if you want to try and do it yourself.

Insulation & Vapor Barrier

What Is This?

This is the insulation under the home that is covered with a plastic mesh type plastic. The vapor barrier is usually black and spans from end to end and side to side.

Types?

Most mobile home vapor barriers are high mil black plastic sheeting.

Benefits & Drawbacks To Each?

The insulation help to keep your utility bills low and adds protection to your plumbing to help keep them from freezing. The vapor barrier assists the insulation plus helps to keep harmful vapors from entering into the living quarters of the mobile home.

How To Check For Problems?

Vapor barriers should not be torn or missing. Sagging vapor barriers could be signs of water leaks and moister damage. If you find that there are taped up holes at or around the bathroom or living room areas of the home you may want to check a little deeper to see if there is a hidden water problem.

How To Fix Those Problems?

You will need to remove all of the damaged insulation and vapor barrier and replace with new.

How Difficult To Fix?

The job to fix this problem is very dirty and dangerous to your health if you do not take the necessary precautions to protect your eyes, lungs and skin. However, this job can usually be completed in one day if you have a couple of workers.

Estimated Cost To Fix?

To replace, or fix, the insulation and vapor barrier on a 76' home (by a professional) will run you somewhere in the $800.00 range. The parts are relatively cheap, if you want to try and do it yourself.

Other Thoughts

If there are openings in this barrier, don't just leave them open. It will cost you money in lost heating and cooling efficiency and will also be a great place for mice and other varmints to get into the home.

Siding

What Is This?

This is the outside part of the home that hides from view all of the framing, pipes, and wires in the wall, plus offers some insulation from outside temperatures' and protection from the outside world.

Types?

Three Types:

1. Metal (looks like corrugated roofing material turned vertical and painted).

2. Vinyl (looks like horizontal vinyl siding)

3. Hardboard/Wooden (looks like paneling and may seem to have the consistency of compressed cardboard).

Benefits & Drawbacks To Each?

Metal is the easiest to get a handle on, has no rot problems, and allows for a myriad of color options. Older homes with metal siding typically will have many dents in the metal which can look unappealing.

Vinyl is the most attractive and modern looking. You can't really paint over it very effectively, as the color is the color. It doesn't rot. However, if a section of it needs replaced it will be hard to match the color as the sun does fade out the vinyl (especially on darker colors).

Wooden (it isn't really wood) is the worst. It frequently is rotted, and the damage can be substantial. It was just a bad idea that some designer had. Try to avoid it if you can. Anything (roof flashing leak, not painting it frequently enough, etc.) can cause it to have the look and feel of rotted, wet cardboard.

How To Check For Problems?

On metal, look for holes, rust, and anything that looks strange. They are pretty much problem free, but may need total cleaning with bleach and repainting.

On vinyl, look for missing pieces of siding, and soft spots in the walls that hold up the vinyl.

On wooden, gosh, where to begin. Look for weak spots, or discoloration throughout every inch of the walls. The soft and rotten spots are usually near the roof or around windows and doors. Most of my biggest home budget killers have been the result of rotted outside trailer walls.

How To Fix Those Problems?

On metal, patch holes or replace sections of the metal with new ones.

On vinyl, replace missing pieces and replace any weak / rotted decking.

On wooden, you will have to replace all rotted sections of wall. And the rot is often <u>much</u> bigger than you thought, once you get the old wood off.

How Difficult To Fix?

Metal: easy. Vinyl: reasonably difficult (unless you are really handy). Wooden: Extremely difficult to impossible without a team and a lot of experience. I think it is the number 1 problem you see when people try to remodel a mobile home themselves.

Estimated Cost To Fix?

Metal will run somewhere in the $20.00 range per section for parts and vinyl will run around $10.00 per piece. The labor will be about double the price of the parts. Wood sided homes will usually cost much more to fix unless the problem is small. I have had jobs run as low as $200.00 and up into the $3,000.00 range. I honestly would not get involved in a house with significant outside wooden siding issues.

Other Thoughts

If you can pull out a ballpoint pen in your pocket and poke a hole through the siding, you have big problems. I've done it many times and it's a clear indicator that you need to move to the next home, unless you're willing to pay to make the necessary repairs.

Skirting

What Is This?

This is the part of the home that hides what is underneath – the blocks, tie-downs, and pipes.

Types?

There have been many different materials used in skirting. The best is vinyl. Others include wood, metal, fiberglass, and masonry.

Benefits & Drawbacks To Each?

Vinyl skirting is the undisputed Cadillac of the industry. If price was no object, everyone would skirt in new vinyl.

After vinyl, all other materials are basically the same. They are successful if they are installed without big gaps and with the visual look of straight lines, and are painted to match the house. Obviously, the more durable the better (fiberglass, for example, is superior to wood). Masonry (brick, cinderblock) is generally a bad idea since you would have to demolish it to move a home, and would even cause problems in re-leveling a home.

How To Check For Problems?

This is purely an aesthetic issue. And most importantly, it really does not matter when you are buying a used home, since whatever skirting is on the home is about to be torn off by you or your mover. Further, skirting really can't be re-used since the height of the home above grade will change when you move the home, so don't plan on using these old pieces in most cases.

This is an issue that you only need to consider upon arrival at the new location.

How To Fix Those Problems?

Since the skirting does not matter on the front end, only when you go to renovate the home at the new destination, let's talk for a minute about what you need to know about installing skirting.

One of the most common rookie mistakes is trying to install vinyl skirting horizontally. It has to be installed <u>vertically.</u> Also, as you will soon learn, the trim package is essential.

How Difficult To Fix?

Installing skirting is not rocket science, but does require a workable knowledge of how to do it. Most people let an installer do this job since it takes a long time and can be hot, nasty work in the blaring sun.

Estimated Cost To Fix?

It costs about $600.00 to skirt a 76' home with new vinyl skirting. If you hire it done count on about $250.00 for installation.

Other Thoughts

The most embarrassing neophyte mistake in skirting is trying to install vinyl skirting horizontally instead of vertically. It just doesn't make sense that you would cut those long horizontal pieces into short vertical ones. Also, in windy areas you will avoid skirting cave-ins if you use some of the reinforcement solutions available from your mobile home parts house.

Stairs

What Is This?

These are the things that allow you to walk from the ground into the front or back door of the mobile home.

Types?

There are basically four materials used in stairs: 1) Wood 2)Fiberglass 3) Concrete and 4) Metal.

There are also an equal number of handrail arrangements.

Benefits & Drawbacks To Each?

Wooden stairs are the most common, but have a lot of drawbacks. First, they don't look very good, and are certainly not an asset to the drive-up appeal of the home. Also they do not hold up well to weather, and will eventually fall apart.

Fiberglass are the best, in our opinion. They look professional, and are hard to damage. Also, because of their weight, they are maneuverable. They also come with professional metal handrails that are infinitely better looking that the wooden ones.

Concrete stairs are good, but they weigh so much that they are nearly impossible to move around.

Metal stairs tend not to be sturdy and rust quickly, causing a run down appearance.

How To Check For Problems?

First of all, like the skirting, the existing stairs will be of no use, in all likelihood, when you get the home to its new location. Unless the height of the home above the ground is identical where it is going, they are just not going to work.

How To Fix Those Problems?

You don't fix stairs. You just replace them. We recommend you buy fiberglass stairs as they look the best, last the longest, are maneuverable, and don't cost that much more than wood.

Be sure, however, to first get the rules on stairs from the city you are in. Some require certain platform sizes and rail specs.

How Difficult To Fix?

Don't fix. Buy new.

Estimated Cost To Fix?

New fiberglass stairs cost about $480.00 with 2 pre-fabricated hand rails.

Other Thoughts

It's funny how some people spend all this time and money renovating a mobile home and then just slap some junky stairs on it. It would be like going to the airport to get on your private jet and having to walk up an old wooden ladder with paint stains all over it and rungs about to break.

Decks

What Is This?

This is the front or back "porch" of the home, which is a platform separating the home from the stairs.

Types?

All the decks that we have ever seen are made of wood. They come in a wide array of sizes and functions, and can be attractively skirted to match the home.

Benefits/Drawbacks?

Decks, generally, add to the appeal of the home from a buyer or renter's perspective. It offers a transition from the stairs to the front or back door, and creates one more area of living space. Additionally, it adds to the "outdoorsy" feel of the home. In some cities, in fact, they are even required.

The important thing to watch in decks is aesthetics. The deck should be professionally done -- level and using good craftsmanship. It should also, if possible, be skirted to match the home. That final touch makes it much more valuable and hides the "junk collection" many tenants store underneath.

How To Check For Problems?

The deck that is on the home, if any, will have to be torn down and removed in order to move the home and, like the stairs, will probably not be re-used. This is an item that you need to budget for and decide on, but don't perform until the home has arrived and is under renovation.

How To Fix Those Problems?

You don't fix a deck, in most cases, you create a new one.

How Difficut To Fix?

Building a deck is a pretty major construction project. Because of the liability if it should collapse, you may want to sub this out to a professional carpenter.

Estimated Cost To Fix?

Depending on the lumber prices and size of the deck, the costs can vary greatly for $300.00 to over a $1,000.00.

Other Thoughts

Many mobile home residents use their deck as an add-on room, storing all of their most unsightly junk right by the front door. It is just another reminder of the unique mindset of some mobile home residents.

Awnings

What Is This?

This is an often decorative item that is found above doors and windows.

Types?

They can be of either metal or fabric.

Benefits & Drawbacks To Each?

Awnings that are clean and not torn are a nice asset to some houses.

However, if they are torn or discolored, they are a negative.

If the home has awnings, then you are probably going to remove them during transport. If they can be easily re-attached upon arrival, and still look good, then go ahead and do it.

If they don't, then throw them away and do not put new ones on. It's a cost you don't need, and they will need perpetual maintenance as they blow off or tear in storms and discolor over time.

How To Check For Problems?

Do the awnings have tears or serious discoloration? If no and they are affixed solidly to the home, then they should be fine.

How To Fix Those Problems?

Don't fix the awnings. If they are still usable, go ahead and continue on. If not, throw them away and do not replace them.

How Difficutlt To Fix?

Don't bother.

Estimated Cost To Fix?

New awnings cost about $50.00 each depending on size and quality.

Other Thoughts

If you feel like you've got to have awnings on the house for aesthetic reasons (and in some cases it does give a house a lot of punch), you should definitely steer towards metal, not fabric. I once got on a kick of trying to do one thing on every home to give it charm. I installed a great looking fabric awning on a home and it really looked quaint – until it ripped in a windstorm about two months later. If you want to give a home a touch of charm, instead of awnings INSTALL VINYL SHUTTERS IN AN ATTRACTIVE COLOR. These are inexpensive, nearly permanent and easy to install.

Carports

What Is This?

This is the, normally metal, roof with four poles that provides shelter to your car(s).

Types?

There are wood ones as well as metal.

Benefits & Drawbacks To Each?

Metal carports, if they come with the house, may be taken apart and moved to the new location. They are rarely pricey to buy (about $1000) so they make a nice asset if you have room for them at the new location.

Wooden carports, cobbled together by the old owner, and probably with a serious lean to them, are usually junk and should be thrown away.

How To Check For Problems?

Metal carports are purchased as kits. They are normally well built and good to transport. They don't need much inspection.

Wooden carports are normally awful and you should not even think of moving them. Even if they are well built, it is usually not worth tearing them down and moving them.

How To Fix Those Problems?

Metal carports may require new posts, since the old ones are sometimes cemented in the ground. Be sure to add this price before you decide whether or not to attempt to move it. Also, be sure to put in a cost to re-erect it.

Wooden ones go in the dumpster.

How Difficult To Fix?

Metal can be fairly easily moved, if you know what you are doing.

Estimated Cost To Fix?

The cost to move and re-erect a metal carport (2 car) is about $200.00. The cost for a new carport will run in the $800.00 to $1,000.00 range.

Other Thoughts

Often you have to remove the carport when you move a mobile home out. Be sure to check the access if you don't plan on moving the carport. You may have to take it down anyway.

Windows

What Is This?

This is what allows the sunshine in and allows you to see out in a mobile home. They are often in every room of the house, and may also have the duty of holding up window air conditioners.

Types?

Mobile home windows are normally made of aluminum frames with glass panes.

Some mobile homes have windows with wooden frames, but this is relatively rare, unless they have been retrofitted later.

Benefits & Drawbacks To Each?

Aluminum windows do not rot, do not warp, and are the best idea. They are relatively easy to obtain in a number of sizes at the mobile home parts store.

Wooden windows rot, warp, and they are not generally a good idea. They do look more like a single family home, though.

How To Check For Problems?

Do the windows have all of their panes? If not, how many are missing or broken and in what sizes?

Do the windows open and close? Check your local laws, because many places require them to function, especially when it's hot out (in case they don't have air conditioning).

Look for rot around the windows that shows signs of leaks.

How To Fix Those Problems?

Missing panes can be replaced with glass or Plexiglas. Replacement is not that difficult.

Aluminum windows that don't function can be replaced by purchasing them from the mobile home parts store. Window installation is fairly difficult for the novice. Rotted areas around windows again require fairly sophisticated handiwork.

How Difficult To Fix?

Panes are easy. Window replacement is not, nor is replacing rotten framing around window. Remember that proper window installation is weather tight –it can't leak or let in.

Estimated Cost To Fix?

Window panes cost about $15.00. A standard aluminum window kit costs approximately $50.00.

Other Thoughts

Don't obsess over window choices if you have to replace a window. The cheapest aluminum framed window will work fine. On broken glass panels, one might want to consider plexiglass—at least you only have to replace it once. Window coverings such as mini blinds and curtains will usually hide any defects anyway.

Screens

What Is This?

This is the wire mesh that keeps the insects out when you open the window or door.

Types?

Metal mesh is the only type I have ever seen on mobile homes. It's held in an aluminum or plastic frame.

Benefits & Drawbacks To Each?

Metal mesh can be easily punctured. This eliminates or reduces its ability to keep out bugs and flies.

Similarly, metal mesh can rust. Rusted screens are an aesthetic problem as they make the home look horrible.

The frames around the screen can become bent, which destroys the ability to be hold in position or keep the bugs out.

How To Check For Problems?

Are the screens all there, or are some of them missing? Make an inventory of number and sizes.

Are the screens rusted?

Are the frames in position, or bent and barely hanging on?

How To Fix Those Problems?

In all cases, a screen with hole in it is easier to replace than fix.

A bent screen is, again, easier to replace than fix. It is very difficult to bend them back to straight.

Rusted screens can be painted, but you have to remove them from the window first.

How Difficult To Fix?

Impossible to fix, except for rust, so don't even try. Buy new screens from the mobile home parts store to replace any that are bent, missing, or have holes in them. Also you may opt to remove all of the screens. Many people do.

Estimated Cost To Fix?

A standard window screen costs $10.00 to $20.00. A screen door costs around $50.00.

Other Thoughts

I have never, ever, had a customer ask about whether or not a mobile home had screens on the windows. I rank it as an absolute non-essential, and I would not spend even one second of time fixing or replacing them. If they are bent or have holes in them I just rip them off and throw them in the dumpster. This is going to be completely up to you and your plans for the home.

Exterior Doors

What Is This?

This is the front door and back door to the mobile home. Every home, for fire safety reasons, should have two <u>working</u> exterior doors.

Types?

They come in several styles:

Standard Mobile Home Doors (foam inside Aluminum or Fiberglass)

1. Metal

2. Hollow wooden

3. Solid wood

4. Obviously, hollow wooden is the least desirable.

Benefits & Drawbacks To Each?

Standard mobile home doors were built for mobile homes and are easy to replace as needed. They fit better than most of the other type of doors and are fairly resilient. They come in many different styles and colors.

Metal doors have a longer life and are harder to punch through. However, they are fairly rare on mobile homes. They normally have foam insulation inside of them. They come fairly much standard on all new mobile homes.

Hollow wooden doors are weak and have poor insulating properties. They are more prone to falling apart and people knocking holes through them.

Solid wooden doors have better insulating properties than hollow wooden (but not as good as metal). They are more durable and harder to punch through. However, both types of wooden doors are subject to warping.

How To Check For Problems?

Both the front and back door must be fully functioning. If not, you may face litigation in case of burglary or fire. They must open, close, lock and have a working dead bolt (check you state and city laws). As long as they do this, the material they are made of is inconsequential except aesthetically.

Check and make sure the doors function well. Additionally, look at the framing around the door to see if there is rot or any other condition that may make operation cease in the near future.

How To Fix Those Problems?

Mobile home front and rear doors in an old home are normally shot. It's a safe bet that you are going to have to replace them both. Fortunately, they are readily available at the mobile home parts store.

Please note that regular household doors will <u>not</u> normally fit a mobile home. Don't make the mistake of buying a regular door at Home Depot or Lowes. I can guarantee you'll be taking it back.

How Difficult To Fix?

When replacing standard mobile home doors, the installation process is definitely achievable for someone with modest skills. By following the manufacturers instructions the whole process of removing the old door and installing the new one should only take about an hour.

Replacing the complete door frame with a house type door is much more intense, and may require hiring a professional.

Estimated Cost To Fix?

Standard mobile home doors cost around $125.00 and up depending on the size and styles chosen. Replacing a standard mobile home door with more of a house type door will have about the same material cost but the labor is more intensive. If possible, splurge a little on the doors, as it makes the first impressions on the customer.

Other Thoughts

I can't reinforce enough that regular house doors like you can buy at Home Depot will <u>not</u> fit on a mobile home. Don't even think about making this most basic of rookie mistakes.

Interior Doors

What Is This?

These are the doors inside the mobile home that give privacy to bedrooms, bathrooms, and the like. They are not built for security.

Types?

Interior doors on mobile homes are ridiculously under built. They have about as much strength as a piece of cardboard – that in fact may be part of what they are made of. They are normally particle wood with some cheap veneer. They are awful.

Benefits & Drawbacks To Each?

Don't try and reengineer the mobile home business and start replacing the bad parts with your own invention. Just buy the correct replacement door from the mobile home parts store and put it in.

Due to their poor construction, it is not unusual to have a hole knocked through every door and the hinges and door knob ripped off. Often the door will by lying on the floor.

How To Check For Problems?

See if all of the doors close and open. If not, you probably need a new door. Fixing the existing door, except in the case of patching holes, is very hard, since there is not much of a place with any strength to screw to.

Inventory the doors and see if they all work.

How To Fix Those Problems?

To cover holes in doors you may glue or screw a piece of sheet metal over the hole and paint the door. Don't obsess with holes in doors, you will have many more if you get the home back.

If the hinges or knobs are broken off, it is often cheaper and easier just to replace the whole door. Remember that regular household doors at Home Depot will <u>not</u> fit a mobile home.

How Difficult To Fix?

Fixing holes is easy. Replacing doors is not that hard. Fixing broken doors is near to impossible.

Estimated Cost To Fix?

Interior doors cost under $50.00 at the mobile home parts supplier.

Other Thoughts

Do not put your own sense of aesthetics into the decorating decision on this topic. If it opens and closes, and stays closed, it's good. Forget the holes and stickers – just patch, paint and go.

Closet Doors

What Is This?

This is the thing that hides the view of the contents of the closet. It can be in the form of a door or sliding panels.

Types?

Mobile home closet doors can be any number of different styles and materials. Since the doors are so weak, most of the doors you will see are retrofitted from a later date. They include wood, metal, sliding panels, sliding mirrors, vertical blinds and beads.

Benefits & Drawbacks To Each?

If you assume that the whole point of the closet door is to block visibility of what's in the closet, then anything that serves the purpose is fine. The key consideration is that the door works and does not have holes through it.

I prefer the sliding mirrored doors on a closet since they make the often tiny mobile home bedroom look larger. But I would not spend 1 cent replacing any doors that are functioning.

Since you will probably repaint the closet doors anyway (except for the mirrored doors), the only part of the closet door function that will irritate your buyer/renter is their ease of opening it and if they can close it securely.

How To Check For Problems?

Open and close each closet door. Doors should not have to be slammed shut to close. And doors should be able to be opened all the way – a sliding closet door that jumps off the track if you open it more than ½ the way is <u>not</u> a working door.

Also inventory holes in doors. Mobile home closet doors are notoriously poor in construction, and even small children can knock holes all the way through them.

How To Fix Those Problems?

Most of the problems with closet doors revolve around their hardware. Faulty tracks and hardware on sliding doors, and bad hinges and knobs on regular doors. All of these can be fairly easily remedied by someone who is moderately handy.

Missing doors can be easily purchased through a mobile home part store. Holes can be patched over and painted.

How Difficult To Fix?

All of the closet door issues are moderately easy to repair. It may take two people to repair the sliding doors due to the awkward way they are installed.

Estimated Cost To Fix?

A mirrored sliding closed door set is about $100.00. Regular closet doors cost about half that much. Replacement hardware is nominal in cost.

Other Thoughts

Sliding closet doors on tracks are one of the worst inventions in all of mobile home land. They never work – not even 30 days after you put the new ones on. Your tenant will rip them off the tracks within two hours of moving in. A better choice is just to use vertical blinds that can be turned to block the view of the contents – or anything that blocks the view but does not slide on tracks. These things derail more than a civil war railroad.

Ceiling

What Is This?

This is the part that hides the framing of the roof from view, offers some degree of temperature insulation, and helps to hide the wires of ceiling fixtures.

Types?

The ceiling of a mobile home is essentially the same in all units, but will differ widely aesthetically. The older homes will have 4' x 14' panels that have the seams covered with plastic strips. Many of the newer homes have drywall ceilings.

Benefits & Drawbacks To Each?

There are no drawbacks to different ceiling types, except aesthetically. Over the years, many different types of ceilings have been used, and some look a little dated today. However, it is not hard to paint the ceilings and modify their look.

How To Check For Problems?

Look for sagging of the ceiling panels. In older homes, this will require replacing those affected sections with new ones. It may also be a sign of rotted rafters that can no longer hold the panels. Bear in mind that some older types of ceiling panels may no longer be in inventory and you will have to match in a slightly different panel, which may have aesthetic issues.

Two additional problems that you may see are signs of water damage and discoloration from smoking in the unit.

How To Fix Those Problems?

In most cases, water marks and smoke discoloration can be fixed with painting with KILZ and then painting over. Sagging sections will require replacement. Rotten rafters will require more significant repairs including rafter replacement.

How Difficult To Fix?

Painting discoloration with KILZ and then painting over it is very easy. It is no different from painting a house interior. Replacing a ceiling section is not that complicated if you take your time and have the correct materials. Fixing a rotten rafter requires know how and if the damage is significant move on to the next house.

Estimated Cost To Fix?

KILZ costs $25.00 a gallon. Paint costs $20.00 a gallon. Ceiling panels cost about $25.00 per section.

Other Thoughts

I have never bought a home with a seriously drooping ceiling. This is often a sign of big problems to come. It costs a bunch to fix, and is the kind of defect that suggest to me that this home has had a lot of abuse and may be nearing the end of its useful life.

Floors

What Is This?

This is the surface you walk on, that is under the carpet or vinyl. Without it, you would fall to the ground.

Types?

There are two types:

1. Solid plywood floors
2. Particle board floors

Benefits & Drawbacks To Each?

Solid plywood floors, especially marine grade plywood is the Cadillac of the industry. It doesn't rot easily, or warp, and is very solid under foot. There is no drawback to it.

Particle board floors are obviously some engineer's idea on how to reduce the cost of building the mobile home. It is a very bad product, and when wet, will turn into mush and have no strength whatsoever. It was a bad design, and I think everyone now agrees.

How To Check For Problems?

Walk the entire floors of the home, every square inch. You are looking for "soft spots" that are weak and make you think you are going to fall through. You are also looking for areas where only the carpet or vinyl is <u>holding you up.</u>

All weak spots will have to be fixed immediately. This means removal of the carpet and pad, or vinyl, in each affected room.

How To Fix Those Problems?

Remove all carpet and pad, or vinyl flooring, from the affected area. Cut a square that removes all non-solid surface, and cut a patch out of solid plywood of the correct thickness (hopefully to match the rest of the flooring. Then replace the carpet or vinyl. Also make sure you found the cause of the leak so you have truly fixed the problem and not just patched it. Some people also (lazily) overlay the floor with new plywood as opposed to only fixing the weak section. This results in floors that are too high and doors that won't clear.

How Difficult To Fix?

Replacing weak spots is a good test of your true desires as a repair-man. Nearly every older home will have them, and they are not fun. It is hard, dirty work that nobody relishes. One mistake many people make is to not cut out a big enough piece of the rotted floor-ing so when they put in the patch it is not supported on all sides.

Estimated Cost To Fix?

If you are patching just a small section or sections of the floor, this job is more labor intensive than cost intensive. One $25.00 sheet of plywood and some screws will do the trick. However, if you have to replace the vinyl or carpet as well, then the costs will be higher.

Other Thoughts

Be sure to walk gingerly when entering a used mobile home. You do not know where you may fall through the floor. Be particularly careful near walls or near discoloration in overhead ceilings. In many cases, only the strength of the carpet is holding you up. When you find a home with rock solid floors, consider buying it immediately. This is a home that probably has no leaks and <u>that</u> is great news.

Carpet

What Is This?

This is the material that covers the floor and has aesthetic, sound deadening, and comfort properties.

Types?

There are many types of carpet. Just a trip to the carpet store will remind you of the almost limitless opportunities.

Not only are there millions of styles, there are also millions or colors to choose from. Mobile homes normally have every style imaginable.

Benefits & Drawbacks To Each?

To be proficient at carpet in a mobile home, you've got to throw your own sense of taste out the window. What you consider tacky is probably perfect as a choice.

Carpet in a mobile home is more like a big, fabric diaper. The family pets go to the bathroom all over it, food is constantly ground into it, and it is never cleaned. As a result, removing the carpet from a mobile home is often the first step in renovating it. Also, it normally has to be removed anyway to get at the soft spots in the floor that have to be patched.

When replacing the carpet in a mobile home, there are three key ideas to remember. First, do not put a pad under the carpet. Why? It helps retain the bad things; dog urine, etc. Second, choose a dark color so it doesn't show filth. Third, always buy the cheapest you can find – the buyer/tenant will most likely destroy it anyway.

How To Check For Problems?

When you buy a used mobile home, you have two choices with the existing carpet. You can steam clean it or replace it.

Look at the existing carpet and see how abused it has been. If there are signs of pet abuse, then it probably can't be cleaned sufficiently – you'll never get the odor out.

Also look for burn marks (from cigarettes) and big holes/tears.

How To Fix Those Problems?

To have an effective steam clean of used carpet, it needs to be dirty from ordinary wear and tear only – tracking dirt, occasional spills, etc. If this is the case, then you can attempt a steam clean. Otherwise you are wasting your time and money.

If the carpet is damaged by pet urine, or has big tears or holes, your only option (and this is 75% of the time) is complete removal. Make this decision on a room-by-room basis. Some rooms can be spared.

How Difficult To Fix?

Steam cleaning cannot remove the odors of pet urine that have soaked into the underlying pad. Since a mobile home has very little airflow, you <u>have</u> to get this out to try and sell or rent this mobile home.

Estimated Cost To Fix?

Steam cleaners can be rented from a store. They cost about $25.00 for a day. Carpet should be purchased from a remnant carpet house, or some other cheap source. Buy a dark color as cheap as you can. Under $5.00 per yard is a good bet here.

Other Thoughts

I once bought a home with hideous midnight blue carpet and gold-painted walls (I mean gold-leaf color, not a form of yellow). It was so ugly that everyone told me that I had to replace the carpet and paint, or sell the home to a Notre Dame Fan. Before I could even decide what to do, someone bought it because they loved the carpet and wall color. The moral: just buy what's the cheapest and go. There is no accounting for taste in mobile home land.

One great invention for mobile homes is the carpet in 14' and 16' widths. Using the proper width of carpet when replacing it will avoid many long seams and is much easier to install.

Pad

What Is This?

This is the spongy material that is laid under the carpet to make it feel more comfortable under foot.

Types?

Pad is all pretty much the same, the big difference being the thickness. Any thickness in a mobile home is too much thickness – the pad acts as a holding ground for spills, pet urine, and the like.

Benefits/Drawbacks?

I can't think of any benefits to carpet pad in a mobile home, as it is the Achilles heal of the carpet concept in a mobile home. Its job in a mobile home is as a big paper towel that soaks up and retains the smells of pet urine, etc.

I would never install pad under carpet in a mobile home.

How To Check For Problems?

If the carpet is shot, it's a given that the pad is no good either. If the carpet is ok then don't worry about the pad. You can't see it anyway. So if the carpet is ok and you just want to steam clean it, just leave the pad alone.

How To Fix Those Problems?

The only way to fix pad is to remove it and throw it away.

If you feel you must replace the pad, then buy the cheapest you can find, and use only a very thin thickness. One other option, if you must, is to buy the carpet that has the thin pad attached to it.

How Difficult To Fix?

Like carpet, pad is not complicated but you have to have a working knowledge of how to do it and the correct tools. If you are not real handy, let a professional install it.

Estimated Cost To Fix?

Pad costs about $2.00 per square yard. Whoever lays the carpet should lay the pad.

Other Thoughts

Think of carpet pad in mobile homes as doggie diapers. You do <u>not</u> want to deliberately put these in a mobile home. You are only asking for trouble if you should get it back.

Vinyl Floor

What Is This?

This is the other flooring option besides carpet, usually found in kitchens and bathrooms, and sometimes entry areas.

Types?

Vinyl comes in many styles and colors. It also comes in basically two types of designs:

1. Large sheet and

2. Individual squares.

Of course, there are many thicknesses and qualities of construction to choose from, too.

Benefits & Drawbacks To Each?

As a mobile home restorer, vinyl aesthetics are the least of your problems. No matter what you choose, it will hardly derail a deal.

More important is the type of vinyl you choose.

The big, seamless sheets of vinyl are probably the better choice in a mobile home since they last longer and are harder to damage.

The individual square designs have serious workability issues in a mobile home. Often, the squares will not stick to the poor quality flooring of particle board, and the weak flexing of the floor will pop them off over time. The press-on type <u>never</u> work. But even with a lot of glue, the squares often look like a checkerboard pretty quickly.

How To Check For Problems?

Look at the existing vinyl. If it is possible, clean it and leave it alone. Don't replace it just for a "look"; if it's undamaged assign that money to something else.

Look for missing squares, tears, and burns. Also, you may have to rip it out anyway to fix soft spots in floors. Kitchens and bathrooms are most notorious for floor problems.

How To Fix Those Problems?

If the existing vinyl is torn or squares are missing, or if the floor has soft spots that need replacement, then you will just have to rip it out and replace it.

Otherwise, clean it aggressively with a strong detergent. You can sometimes patch missing squares or tears with new vinyl pieces of a similar style and color.

How Difficult To Fix?

Replacement of vinyl is not rocket-science, but does require some knowledge of how to do it and the right tools. It can often be dirty and back-breaking work, but the amount of vinyl normally is pretty small.

Estimated Cost To Fix?

New vinyl costs about $150.00 for a kitchen and $50 for a bathroom. Buy cheap stuff, since the new buyer/tenant will probably destroy it anyway. Choose a pattern that disguises abuse (very busy pattern).

Other Thoughts

I have never, ever seen a vinyl floor with press-on squares that has all of the squares. Clearly, this is a really bad design in mobile homes. You are much better off with large sheets of vinyl. Also, when replacing vinyl make sure you are attaching it to a clean and smooth surface without screw heads. Use Bondo or other floor patch to cover all seams and screw/nail heads.

Interior Walls

What Is This?

This is the stuff that hides the view of the wires, pipes and studs in the wall, and creates privacy, as well as deadens sound.

Types?

Interior walls vary based on the age of the home and what was in vogue at that time. Early mobile homes have expensive tongue-in-grove wood paneling in some cases. Other old homes have that fake "Sears" paneling form the 1970's . Some of the other types include vinyl covered panels and more recently drywall.

Benefits & Drawbacks To Each?

The whole point of interior walls in a mobile home is pretty basic: to hide the wires, pipes and 2" x 2"s in the wall, and create a little privacy. As a result, <u>any</u> type of interior wall material is fine as long as it has no rot or holes in it.

Given that statement, all of the various types: solid paneling, fake paneling or drywall are all about equal. Obviously, solid wood paneling is the most desirable, followed by drywall. But in many cases, the fake wood paneling is the least maintenance intensive.

How To Check For Problems?

Walk the entire interior of the home, looking for rotted wall sections or holes through the wall. The average home will have many, many holes. Signs of rot will be discolored areas, or soft spots, normally around windows, exterior doors, and weak spots in floors.

How To Fix Those Problems?

Rotted areas should be replaced with whatever offers the closest match to existing drywall or paneling. Don't obsess on getting it just right, the customer will never notice, and probably knock a hole through it in the first few days, anyway.

Holes can be covered with a sheet of thin sheet metal, or veneer. Then just paint over the patch. Everything else is fixed with paint and putty.

How Difficult To Fix?

Replacing drywall / paneling, or patching holes is very easy. You can buy all of the parts you need at Lowes, Home Depot, or a mobile home parts supply house.

Estimated Cost To Fix?

A sheet of drywall costs under $10.00 and a sheet of fake paneling costs about $15.00. Patches are $5.00 or less.

Other Thoughts

Tape, bed, match the texturing – heck no! Patch, paint and go. The walls will get destroyed the minute you turn over the keys. Decals, gum, posters with push pins, marks-a-lot and fists through walls are all part of the plan once you are out of the room. Don't waste your time.

Counters

What Is This?

These are the things that hold up your sinks, and offer space for the preparation of food in the kitchen.

Types?

Counters are found in two rooms of a mobile home:

1. Kitchen
2. Bathrooms

The materials that counters are made of in a mobile home are many. The most common is Formica.

Benefits & Drawbacks To Each?

The whole point of the counter in a mobile home is strictly utilitarian. As long as it can hold up the sinks and allow you to make a sandwich without crashing down to the floor, then all is well. Aesthetics are seldom a big issue in mobile homes.

Formica is most common, and is perfectly suitable for all mobile homes. Granite and marble counters in mobile homes are ridiculous and out of place. Don't confuse a custom home with mobile home.

How To Check For Problems?

Look at the counters. Do they touch the wall? Are the sinks fitting in them without big gaps? Are they warped? Push on them, are they solid and stable? Also, see if they just lift off. Sometimes, when retrofitted, the owner doesn't even bother to tack them down.

Look at the discoloration or flaws in the counters. These will need to be mitigated with paint or patching.

How To Fix Those Problems?

If the counters are rotted, warped, or not cut right, you will need to replace them. You can, in most cases, have the counter cut to your specification and all you have to do is install it.

All patches/repairs/touch-ups can be accomplished fairly easily as long as you do not obsess on the outcome. Most customers will not notice and it certainly will not preclude a sale/rental.

Usually rather than replacing the countertops you can get by with removing the old caulking, placing a new bead of caulk and adding new trim pieces around the edges.

How Difficult To Fix?

Replacing counters is not that hard, but will require some degree of knowledge and tools. It will also require help to install, because they are often heavy and awkward to lift. Painting/patching is pretty easy.

Estimated Cost To Fix?

A sample kitchen counter, new, costs $100.00 and up. A bathroom counter costs $50.00 and up.

Other Thoughts

The key with countertops to make them last is to take care of them. Make sure you keep the seams sealed and the edges caulked. If you start letting water in behind them or under the formica it won't be long before they rot out and you have to replace them.

In bathrooms one of the greatest inventions was the countertop with the preinstalled sink. If you have to replace a bathroom countertop, go this route as it looks good, is easy to replace, and lasts longer.

Cabinets

What Is This?

These are the built-ins that allow you to store things in the kitchen, bath and sometimes above the washer/dryer connection.

Types?

There are a wide range of materials that cabinets may be made of in a mobile home. These include solid wood, wood veneer over pressed wood, and metal. You may also see plastic that has been retrofitted in some older homes.

Benefits & Drawbacks To Each?

It's not so much what the cabinet is made of that makes for problems – more how it is attached to the wall. It is hard to get a solid hold on anything in a mobile home, so your primary concern is if the cabinets are anchored effectively.

Of all the cabinet materials, obviously, solid wood is best. It is more durable, and is favored by your customers.

Metal has good longevity and low weight, so it is also a good option, although not as well received by customers.

Anything in a mobile home made of pressed wood is lousy since moisture turns it to mush.

If the cabinets are <u>missing</u>, that is a pretty big expense to replace.

How To Check For Problems?

Open up the cabinet doors and see if they work. If not, see if they can be fixed easily. If the hinges are ripped off and the wood is rotted out then it will be harder to fix and probably replacing is your best option. Missing doors can be replaced as long is there is a place to attach them to.

The key thing to check for is if the cabinet is securely fastened to the wall. Look at it from the side and see if it is detaching from the wall. Pull a little bit on it to see if it has a solid feel, or if you could pull it off the wall yourself. Also look at the bottoms of each cabinet for water damage.

How To Fix Those Problems?

Weak or rotted cabinet bottoms can be easily fixed by overlaying the existing floor of the cabinet. Wobbly or ill-fitting doors can be fixed by adjusting hinges and/or locks.

One of the hardest fixes in the mobile home is re-attaching cabinets to walls. Often, the framing is too weak in the wall to support the cabinets. If this is the case, the cost could be extremely high, and will require a professional.

How Difficult To Fix?

Attaching the cabinets to walls is tough. Often, you are better advised to buy standing cabinets from Lowes or Home Depot and not even attempt to re-attach them. Such kits do not require any walls to hold them up because the weight is on the floor.

Estimated Cost To Fix?

The cost to repair cabinet bottoms, or re-attach doors is slight. Missing doors can be cobbled together from close look-a-likes or sealed shut. Replacing cabinets is very expensive, as is anchoring them to the wall, in the range of $500.00 to several thousand dollars.

Other Thoughts

I used to spend big money re-attaching cabinets that were falling off walls. Today, I just install pre-made cabinets from Home Depot or Lowes that rest on the floor. They are cheap and nobody complains.

Appliances

What Is This?

These are the devices in the kitchen that allow for cooking (range/oven, microwave), refrigerator, and sometimes washer/dryer.

Types?

Standard kitchen appliances are oven/range, refrigerator and microwave. Dishwashers are fairly rare in older mobile homes, as are disposals. Some mobile homes have connections also for washers and dryers.

Benefits & Drawbacks To Each?

There is no reason to fret over the best appliances because whatever you install will probably be trashed or stolen upon the exit of your buyer/tenant. So if you must install them, buy only the cheapest you can buy. You can buy used, but they are often prone to break down pretty soon after purchase. In today's world of cheap new appliances, you are probably better off to find the cheapest of each type at a store. Sometimes "scratch and dent" appliance stores will have cheap units.

You are also better off to sell/rent mobile homes without appliances. This gets a major source of repair issues out of your hair, since they have to provide and repair their own. They can always rent these things from a local rent-to-own store. Appliance problems are a major source of repair and maintenance calls to you, and are easily stolen.

How To Check For Problems?

If your range/oven or other appliance is not working, then just remove it. The cost to fix such items today is normally more than the cost to replace them with new. Appliances have become almost a "disposable" commodity.

If you remove an appliance, I would urge you strongly not to replace it – let the tenant get their own. It will save you a <u>huge</u> amount of money and grief.

How To Fix Those Problems?

Remove all non-functioning appliances. Replace with cheap new ones if you feel you must, but you are better off letting the buyer/tenant get their own.

Be sure to get the right type of appliance for the home. If the range/oven is electric you <u>must</u> get an electric. Don't buy a gas appliance for an electric hook-up, or visa versa.

How Difficult To Fix?

Appliances are extremely hard to fix. Don't even think about trying to do so yourself. They are too cheap to buy to make any sense of repairing all but the most expensive ones.

Estimated Cost To Fix?

A new range/oven costs about $225.00. A new refrigerator cost about $350.00. A dishwasher costs around $225.00.

Other Thoughts

Let the tenant go to the rental store for these. You are a fool if you keep fixing and replacing them – they will turn up missing or broken on every turn-over of tenants. When I stopped supplying them, nobody even asked about it.

Central A/C:

What Is This?

This is the device that enables the house to cool down below the temperature of the outside air as well as remove the humidity out of the inside air.

Types?

Most central a/c systems are fairly identical, using an indoor coil system and an outdoor unit. There are, however, some areas of the U.S. where you find a "swamp cooler" system that uses a slightly different technology.

Benefits & Drawbacks To Each?

A good central A/C system is the Cadillac of the cooling industry. It keeps a house consistently cool in every room, is quiet, and fairly energy efficient. It can be pretty expensive though, costing about $2,500 or more to install. And within the a/c world, there are many different brands and energy efficiency ratings to understand. As long as a mobile home central a/c system is working, don't even think about replacing it. Your buyer/tenant only cares that it works and keeps the place cool.

Swamp coolers use a technology of flowing water to blow air over cool water into the house. This system works well in dry and hot climates. It does not work in humid climates because it actually adds humidity as one of its functions.

How To Check For Problems?

Inspect the coils (in the house) and the outdoor unit for the need to be cleaned, as well as wiring issues. Turn on the system and see if it blows cold air and, if it does, how cold is the air?

Don't be discouraged if the outdoor a/c unit is missing. They are normally stolen by the ex-tenant or mobile home mover. It is rare to find a working one that comes with an older home.

How To Fix Those Problems?

Unless you are trained as an a/c repairman, you will have to use a professional to analyze why the a/c system in not blowing cold, or to install a new system.

As we will discuss later you may want to replace the central a/c system with a window a/c system. It is a lot cheaper!

How Difficult To Fix?

Very. Unless you are a certified a/c repairman, don't even think about it.

Estimated Cost To Fix?

A new central a/c system costs about $2,500.00 installed. That's a lot of money. You may want to consider a window a/c system if you are in a humid climate. If you are in a dry climate then a swamp cooler will only cost about $300.00 and is much cheaper to operate.

Other Thoughts

Unless you have a real good argument, I would convert to window air when the A/C system dies. They are cheap and, if stolen, cheap to replace.

Window A/C:

What Is This?

This is a piece of equipment that fits in the window and is used to cool the house below the temperature of the outside air.

Types?

There are many types of window a/c and different types of strength of cooling capability (each one pulls more energy). There is also a window heat/air system that may be beneficial.

Benefits & Drawbacks To Each?

The first consideration in examining window a/c as an option is how much power the home is wired to handle, and where the a/c will plug in – does it have the correct plug. The last thing you want to do is create the danger of electrical fire and, since a/c units draw a huge amount of power, this is a major consideration.

Most, but not all, 100 amp houses can handle two units, a big window unit and another small bedroom unit. Before you even think about this option, you may want the home checked by a licensed electrician to see what the capability is, and where the plugs are or could be.

Also, before you begin to ponder window a/c, look at your furnace. If it is not working, you may want to consider a combination a/c and heating unit.

How To Check For Problems?

If there are already window a/c units in the house, see if they work. If they are blowing cold, and the thermostats work, then you are fine. If it isn't broken, don't fix it. If the unit does not work, then trash it, since they are cheaper to buy new than to fix.

How To Fix Those Problems?

If the window a/c is broken, throw it away. Do not call a repairman – they cost too little new to waste money fixing an old unit.

How Difficult To Fix?

Extremely. Don't do it. They are a source of electrical fire if you do it wrong, and contain pollutants to the environment.

Estimated Cost To Fix?

A big window air unit costs $300.00. A small "bedroom" unit costs $100.00. A big window heat/air unit costs $400.00.

Other Thoughts

I love window A/C. I never thought about them until a mobile home renovator suggested I try it. I'm hooked. They are a simple system, unlike central A/C, and easy to use. I even think that tenants like them – they make a nice calming noise at night, and when you are really hot you can stand right in front of them for a quick thrill. I have nothing bad to say about them. My only caution is to not buy used and renovated units. They do not seem to last very long, and cost about the same as new ones.

Window Heat/Air

What Is This?

This is a device that fits in the window and lets you cool down the house in the summer, and heat it in the winter.

Types?

There are many different brands of window heat/air. The important issue is the amount of power they have and draw, and what the house is able to withstand in the form of electricity used.

Benefits & Drawbacks To Each?

A window heat/air, in the appropriate circumstances, is a godsend over the cost of a central a/c and furnace system. Particularly in a small house, this one device, which costs about $500.00 is $3,000.00 less than a new furnace and central a/c system.

How To Check For Problems?

If the problem is a broken A/C and furnace or if you are putting a home with a gas furnace in an all electric park, then a window hear/air unit may be the solution.

Make sure to consult with a licensed electrician to see if the home can handle it electrically, and to have the plug identified or installed for it.

How To Fix Those Problems?

One large window heat/air can often successfully cool and heat an entire mobile home, especially if the home is smaller. Of equal importance is the geographical location of the home. It needs to be in an area of moderate summers and winters, with rare temperature extremes to work efficiently.

The tremendous cost advantage of this system may make it worth a try.

How Difficult To Fix?

In an environment where a central a/c and furnace may cost $3,500 installed, a window heat/air is a bargain – the cost difference might buy you a second mobile home!

Estimated Cost To Fix?

A large window heat/air unit costs around $400.00.

Other Thoughts

I am a huge fan of this product. I think it is one of the best cost-cutting measures you have if the central systems are broken. I have never had complaining from a tenant over them.

Furnace

What Is This?

This is the equipment that heats the home above the temperature of the outside air.

Types?

All furnaces work on the same system, and are pretty much identical. The important thing to note is what powers them: is it natural gas, propane, or all-electric. Wood is not a legal option and if retrofitted in your home, remove it at once.

Benefits & Drawbacks To Each?

A working furnace is a working furnace, don't obsess over its brand or model. Make sure, however, that the furnace is safe and in good working order, and powered by the appropriate energy source.

Also remember that different parks have different availabilities of heating options. For example, an all-electric park has no natural gas. This means your gas furnace is useless unless propane can be brought in.

Also, make extremely sure that the furnace is what is intended for the house. I have seen many all-electric furnaces put in mobile homes that were only engineered for gas, and this could cause a major fire.

How To Check For Problems?

Have the furnace thoroughly checked by a licensed repairman. There is <u>way</u> too much liability here to do it yourself. This is the number one source of fire in mobile homes.

If the system is broken, or does not fit the design of the house, you need to have it removed immediately. You do not need the risk of liability if you keep a dangerous furnace.

How To Fix Those Problems?

If a furnace is broken, fix or replace it, using a licensed repairman/installer. If the home was designed for a gas unit, be sure to put a gas unit in it. You do <u>not</u> want to overload your electrical system.

You may also want to consider a window heat/air unit, which we just described as a low cost alternative to a furnace.

How Difficult To Fix?

Only a licensed technician should work on a furnace. Period.

Estimated Cost To Fix?

A new furnace costs about $1,500.00 to $2,000.00 (Gas is usually about $300 more than electric).

Other Thoughts

These things scare me. When you think of the enormous heat they produce, I am terrified to use them if they are not 100% perfect, and few are. If you want to burn a house down, this is the best way to do it – use a bad furnace.

Ducts

What Is This?

These are the "canals" that direct the hot and/or cold air from the furnace and/or air conditioner to the rooms of the house.

Types?

The most common type of duct work is normally box type and made of metal. In some newer homes, you will find more modern flexible ducting.

Benefits & Drawbacks To Each?

There is no decision to be made here except whether or not what is currently there is working. In most cases, everything works except there may be separations in the venting that causes a lot of the air to leak out under the trailer.

You may also want to consider cleaning out the ductwork, or replacing the grates.

How To Check For Problems?

There is no way to check for problems without turning the system on. As a result, this may be one of the last repairs that you do. Also, in the event that you decide to convert the home from central heat or air to window heat/air, the ductwork has no further purpose and there is no reason to waste your time until you know if you will be even using the ducts or not.

How To Fix Those Problems?

The normal procedure on leaking ducts is to either push the pieces of the ductwork back together and secure, or wrap these leaking areas with tape or some other manner.

Replacing duct grates is super easy – if you can use a screwdriver, you can do that job. Often, you can just pull out the grates, clean them, and spray paint them and they will look new.

How Difficult To Fix?

Fixing ductwork is normally just a matter of labor and maybe a roll of tape. To hire this done it will be in the $100.00 to $200.00 range.

Estimated Cost To Fix?

This is mostly a labor intensive job with nominal costs for parts.

Other Thoughts

If you ever take the grates off and reach into the ducts, you will think you are a pirate – they are often filled with coins, mostly pennies. Of course, they can also be filled with all kinds of nasty stuff, so be sure to wear gloves. We once found a dead raccoon stuffed in a vent -- it had crawled in from under the trailer and could not get out!

Hot Water Heater

What Is This?

This is the machine that turns regular water into hot water.

Types?

They are all basically the same but with two important differences:

What capacity are they (how much hot water can they create)?

What powers them (electricity or gas)?

Benefits & Drawbacks To Each?

Your home is built to have either a gas powered or electric powered hot water heater. You must re-install whatever the home is set up to handle. Don't put the wrong type in your home by mistake.

On capacity, like all things the bigger the better. However, check the size of the compartment that it fits in and see how big of a unit will fit. Often, mobile homes are set up only for smaller type capacities. Again, you pretty much have to go with what the home was built to handle.

How To Check For Problems?

Look for signs of leaks if the water is not turned on. If you see discoloration or rot, then it's a good bet the hot water heater is leaking. In any event, since it is not that expensive and is a common leak and repair issue, go ahead and replace it unless you can see that it was newly retrofitted. If you don't, you probably will have to anyway shortly, and it is easier before you renovate the house.

How To Fix Those Problems?

Replace the hot water heater and while you are doing that, go ahead and fix the floor underneath, which is probably bad and weak.

How Difficult To Fix?

You need a licensed plumber to replace the hot water heater, on the floor itself, it's your choice whether to do it yourself or hire it done.

Estimated Cost To Fix?

A hot water heater will cost about $250.00. Installations should run about $100.00 additional.

Other Thoughts

Mobile Home water heaters are not usually the same as those that go in a site built home. They are typically narrower and taller. If you put in the wrong type of water heater you may end up causing a fire or being red tagged by the code inspectors.

Electrical Box

What Is This?

This is the box where your breakers are, that is the central spot from where all of the wiring in the home emanates from.

Types?

There are several different manufacturers and types of breakers and fuses in the electrical box, but they all serve the same function. Nobody, short of an electrician, knows or cares about the brand.

Benefits & Drawbacks To Each?

The brand and its plusses or minuses is immaterial.

The only important thing is safety – is the box functioning as intended, is it big enough to handle the load and has it been retrofitted in an inappropriate way?

If the electrical box has been compromised in any way, or is not functioning as intended, the result may be fire.

How To Check For Problems?

Have a licensed electrician examine the box. You may, as an untrained observer see immediate signs of abuse, like wires that appear to have been added in, or a new box that was poorly installed, but let a professional give you the real grade card.

How To Fix Those Problems?

If the box is wrong, you need to have a licensed electrician immediately remove and/or fix it. The downside to the box being bad is a major fire.

How Difficult To Fix?

Unless you are a certified, licensed electrician, you have no business messing with the box. Ever.

Estimated Cost To Fix?

To replace a box may cost $500.00 to $750.00. To not fix it may cost you your entire house to a fire, plus the liability of damage to people or their belongings.

Other Thoughts

Has someone tampered with the electrical box? Then move on to the next house. This is a very bad sign. If they had the guts to rig the power box, then they may have rigged almost anything, and the house is probably filled with latent defects.

Electrical Wiring

What Is This?

This is the stuff that runs from your electrical panel through the walls of the house to the outlets and appliances.

Types?

Wiring is normally copper. But what it should not be, although is in many houses, is aluminum. Aluminum wiring is extremely dangerous as it can overheat and cause fires. You probably have seen or read or heard about the dangers of aluminum wiring.

Benefits & Drawbacks To Each?

Wiring is wiring, unless it is aluminum.

Aluminum is extremely dangerous, yet was a common type of wiring installed by manufactures of mobile homes several years ago from about 1967 to 1971. In older homes, especially with the many switches and plugs that may have been replaced over the years, the problem is very dangerous.

For all other types of wiring, if the home is treated right, it never needs repair or replacement.

How To Check For Problems?

Have a licensed electrician check for aluminum wiring. If you have it, you must make a business decision of whether or not to go forward with buying the home. It is way to expensive to try and re-wire the home into something other than aluminum, so don't even think about it.

For all other types of wiring, check each plug to see if it is working, as well as each switch. A non-functioning switch or plug may be a fire hazard.

How To Fix Those Problems?

If the house has aluminum wiring, you have to make a business decision on whether to buy it or not. Personally, I won't buy a mobile home with aluminum wiring.

On the switches and plugs, I use a certified electrician only to fix. If you have a good knowledge of electricity, the decision is up to you to fix it yourself, but there is a lot of liability to consider.

How Difficult To Fix?

Impossible – the cost is too great, if the problem is aluminum wiring.

Switches and plugs are relatively easy for an electrician to fix.

Estmated Cost To Fix?

A full rewire job is going to run in the $2,000.00 range and up. A fortune. Don't even think about it, if the issue is aluminum wiring. Plugs and switches are mostly labor cost only – the parts are cheap.

Other Thoughts

If you see extension cords being used to move electricity between rooms, or to avoid certain outlets, then this is not the home for you, unless you are an electrician and have access to free labor. This is a terrible sign of latent defects, and a lot of liability.

Light Fixtures

What Is This?

These are the ceiling fixtures that provide light to each room, as well as any other light source turned on with a switch.

Types?

The most common is the ceiling fixture, which normally has two horizontal bulbs hidden under a glass or plastic decorative "bowl". Other types include wall sconces and bathroom "light strips".

Benefits & Drawbacks To Each?

If they work, they are fine. The bulbs should be hidden, so if the "bowl" is missing, that fixture is not really satisfactory.

If they spark or flicker, they should be replaced. There is too much liability with electricity.

How To Check For Problems?

Do they turn on an off, and have all their pieces? If yes, then they are fine. If not, they have to be replaced.

You cannot check the operation until you have power connections. This is often one of the last things in the home to be replaced.

How To Fix Those Problems?

You don't fix ceiling fixtures, you just replace them. Why? Because they are so darn cheap. Thanks to overseas labor, you can buy every fixture in the house for the price of one hour of a repair technician.

How Difficult To Fix?

Let a certified electrician do it. There is a ton of liability if you put them in wrong and burn the house down. Plus, you would not be the first amateur to get killed by electrocution.

Estimated Cost To Fix?

Fixtures cost about $15.00 each. Have the electrician put them in when he is there to check out the wiring to save money on the installation cost.

Other Thoughts

Anything more than a simple light bulb hanging from a wire is O.K. in a mobile home. Buy the cheapest thing at Home Depot and move on.

Water Lines

What Is This?

This is the piping that allows you to have cold and hot water in the mobile home. It supplies the kitchen, bathroom(s) and sometimes the washer/dryer connections.

Types?

Hopefully PVC or a derivative, or copper or metal. What you don't want is the "black pipe" that was the subject of a class-action lawsuit years ago.

Benefits & Drawbacks To Each?

The water line construction that is truly bad is "black plastic". It's easy to spot – it looks like PVC except it is black. Of the other types, PVC is the best for longevity, as is copper.

Black plastic, which was part of a class action suit, is bad stuff. It is very brittle and breaks easily. As part of the class action suit settlement, you may be able to recoup the cost of replacing the black plastic pipe if you follow the appropriate steps. You will need to contact and follow those steps to get reimbursed, if any money is available.

How To Check For Problems?

Connect the water and look for leaks or water sources that won't turn on. Look under the trailer and see if you see water dripping, or running, from anywhere underneath the mobile home. Look for black plastic pipe.

How To Fix Those Problems?

Black plastic pipe requires full replacement. Without some form of reimbursement, it may be too expensive to contemplate.

The other leak or flow issues can be remedied by a licensed plumber or yourself if you're handy.

How Difficult To Fix?

Black plastic is impossible without total replacement.

The other issues are not hard if you know what you are doing. Access to the pipes is the hardest part, as it may require crawling under the home, or cutting out drywall or flooring to access and correct the problem.

Repairs are pretty cheap. A full replacement could cost $800.00 or more.

Other Thoughts

"Out of sight, out of mind" does not apply here. Water leaks can cause all kinds of problems to floors, walls, etc. Don't make a rookie mistake – get the water line connected and up and running and check for leaks <u>before</u> you do any interior work. You do not want to be chopping out your new walls, or wrecking your new floors.

One sure trap will be when you go to buy a mobile home in the dead of winter and the temperatures are such that they are freezing. If the home has not been winterized you will be asking for problems when you turn the water on. This is always something to look out for.

Sewer Lines

What Is This?

These are the lines that run from the sinks, showers, baths, and toilets to carry the fluids to the sewer line.

Types?

This is one area where problems are few. There are several different types of sewer piping, PVC being the best, but the sewer gets so little use in a mobile home that it is seldom a big deal no matter how it is piped.

Benefits & Drawbacks To Each?

If the sewer is flowing with no leaks, don't worry about it. The type of pipe is immaterial.

How To Check For Problems?

The only real way to test is to flush the toilet, run the shower, turn on the faucet, and look for leaks inside and under the mobile home.

How To Fix Those Problems?

Leaks will need to be fixed by patching or replacing pipe. The biggest problem I have found is what happens to a perfectly good sewer pipe if abandoned for a lot of years. During that time, all of the stuff in the pipe turns hard like concrete, and may cause it to be near impossible to fix or unclog.

How Difficut To Fix?

If you are handy, you can probably fix a lot of sewer issues yourself. If not, a plumber can do it. Most sewer line problems will occur in the p-traps and from the toilet to the main sewer line. A quick snaking or repair will solve most problems.

Estimated Cost To Fix?

Not a lot. The bulk of the expense is labor, since you have to crawl under the home to fix it in most instances.

Other Thoughts

These are rarely ever big problems. The thing I have disliked the most is when the sewer has puddled up under the home and you have to climb under there to make the repair.

Gas Lines

What Is This?

These are pipes that connect the natural gas or propane service to your furnace, range/oven, or hot water heater.

Types?

Gas lines may be made of metal or polypipe (plastic) construction. They should never be made of copper (explosion hazard).

Benefits & Drawbacks To Each?

A gas line is a gas line and if it works, then that's fine, as long as it is made of a type of pipe that is safe for gas.

Some people in the past have retrofitted copper as gas lines and that is dangerous and should be replaced.

How To Check For Problems?

All gas lines should be pressure tested by a licensed gas plumber. Make sure the plumber is licensed for gas, not just a regular plumber.

Because gas is extremely volatile, there can be no leaks of any type in the system.

If you are going to replace any gas devices, such as hot water you should do so at the same time the gas plumber is there to save money.

How To Fix Those Problems?

Only a licensed gas plumber should work on gas lines. Period. If you do this yourself, and the house blows up, which it can, the liability will wipe you out – maybe even send you to prison.

You can find licensed gas plumbers through the yellow pages.

How Difficult To Fix?

Extremely, if you are not a professional – do not even try. The liability is way too great.

Estimated Cost To Fix?

Gas plumbers charge $100.00 an hour on average. To check out your system and fix a few leaks should run about $175.00.

Other Thoughts

Leaks in this department are normally on connections with the lines and appliances and the furnace. The lines are normally O.K. themselves.

Tubs

What Is This?

This is the fixture that fills with water for baths, or additionally may be used as the base for the shower.

Types?

Tubs come in a number of styles, but the most common is the shower/tub combo. They are normally not especially big or well made.

Benefits & Drawbacks To Each?

You pretty much have to replace what is already there, since normally there is a wall on either side of the tub. As a result, you don't have much, or any, selection.

One choice you do have is color. Obviously, you are better off replacing a broken tub with a new one that has a neutral color. If the old tub was mustard yellow, don't feel obligated to put that same color back. Off-white is probably a better choice.

Most residential tubs from Lowes or Home Deport will <u>not</u> fit in a mobile home, so you need to order it from a mobile home parts supplier.

How To Check For Problems?

Often the best way to find the problems in mobile home tubs is to step inside of them and see what happens. Often, the addition of the weight will tell the story – cracks are suddenly visible, as are flooring issues. Also look for big gaps or breaks where the tub meets the walls.

At a minimum, normally the hardware (faucet, handles, etc). will need to be replaced for non-functioning or rust issues.

How To Fix Those Problems?

Hardware is reasonably easy to replace if you're handy. However, replacing the tub is normally pretty complicated, if you want to do it right. Also, be sure to replace or fix the floor before you set a new tub, since you will have to rip it back out again.

Often, you will need to install a tub/shower enclosure kit, again available at the mobile home part supply house.

How Difficult To Fix?

Fixtures are not that bad, if you know about plumbing. The entire tub and enclosure is pretty hard if you have not done one before, or are not handy. When you are replacing the tub/shower enclosure make sure that you buy the set made for a remodel which come in two pieces. It can be impossible to put a one piece unit into a small bathroom.

Estimated Cost To Fix?

A new tub/shower enclosure kit is about $300.00.

Other Thoughts

The key with the enclosure around the tub and shower is to make sure it does not allow water to leak between it and the walls. Once again, a good caulking job will do the trick.

I once went into a home for sale and found the tub filled with snakes who were bathing in the water that came through the hole in the ceiling. At least that house was vacant. I looked at another house that had suds all over the tub – and it was occupied!

Toilets

What Is This?

This is the fixture that allows you to go to the bathroom.

Types?

A toilet is a toilet. Other than designer touches and some better flushing mechanisms, the function is always the same.

Benefits & Drawbacks To Each?

Buy the cheapest toilet you can find. This is the only thing to remember. You will not believe the abuse mobile home people put on toilets.

They rip the seats off, the covers off, and break the toilet free from the floor just in the regular course of business. It is a safe bet that you will have to replace the toilet every time you lose a tenant.

This is one time you can be especially thankful to the third world for building toilets so cheap – they cost today about 75% less than twenty years ago.

How To Check For Problems?

Just look at the toilet. Would you use it if it was in your house? If the answer is no, then just replace it. It sounds stupid, but it is cheaper to replace it than clean it today. You probably can't find someone to clean it for $25, but you can buy one for about double that. Also look at the way it is affixed to the floor. Is there a leak between the main seal and the toilet (a sign that the wax ring needs replacing)? Also, is it loose and rocking side to side?

How To Fix Those Problems?

On all aesthetic issues, just replace the toilet. If it is rocking back and forth, it is probably a sign that the floor is rotted and needs replacing. Normally, the floor in the bathroom always needs patching/replacing and the time to do that is when the toilet is removed.

How Difficult To Fix?

Replacing a toilet is mundane for the handy individual who has a working knowledge of plumbing. For the rest of us, it is better left to a plumber.

Estimated Cost To Fix?

A new, cheap toilet costs $50.00. This is one item that any toilet from Lowes or Home Depot will fit – it does not have to come from a mobile home parts dealer.

Anytime you install a new or old toilet don't skimp on putting in new wax ring. That $1.00 part is about the best plumbing supply money can buy.

Other Thoughts

If you would rather clean than replace a toilet that has seen more action than a B-17 bomber, then my hat is off to you. I can find better uses for my time, when you consider you can buy a whole new toilet at Home Depot for about $50.00 – and it will even have a seat!

Sinks

What Is This?

This is the basin that collects water from the faucet and puts it in the drain.

Types?

There are many different types of sinks aesthetically, and as many fixture choices to match.

The two rooms that have a sink are the bathroom and the kitchen.

Benefits & Drawbacks To Each?

A sink is a sink. If you must replace it, be sure to buy one that already fits in the hole cut in the counter.

It is not that often that you have to replace the sink in a mobile home. They seem to hold up pretty well.

Often the sink is replaced upon replacing the counter top.

As usual, buy the cheapest one that you can that fits the space.

How To Check For Problems?

Sink problems are mostly aesthetic. That's not to say that there cannot be issues with leaks from drains, but that falls under plumbing. As long as the sink collects water and directs it to the drain, it's done its job.

If the sink looks O.K., and it would have to be in <u>really</u> bad shape to need replacing, then you can move on to another problem.

It is common, however, to need to replace the faucet and handles.

How To Fix Those Problems?

Faucet and handles are readily available most everywhere. They do not have to be mobile home specific, unless your sink is. If the sink is marred with a ton of nicks and scratches, you can sometimes paint them.

Full replacement of a sink is probably not that hard for the handy person with experience, but is seldom warranted.

How Difficult To Fix?

Faucet and handle replacement is not too bad if you are handy.

Replacing the whole sink is not outside the range of a handy person with plumbing experience, but is a last resort.

Estimated Cost To Fix?

A new sink costs about $40.00. The faucet and handles cost about $20.00.

Other Thoughts

Spray paint over the porcelain or stainless steel? I've done it a hundred times. They renovate claw-foot bathtubs with acrylic paint – why not some old sinks. I've never had a complaint.

Fireplaces

What Is This?

This is the fixture that allows you to burn wood, or some other fuel for either aesthetic or heating purposes.

Types?

This is easy. IF IT'S NOT ORIGINAL TO THE HOUSE, DOES NOT HAVE THE CORRECT VENTING OR INSTALLATION, THEN RIP IT OUT. PERIOD.

Benefits/Drawbacks?

This thing can burn your house down, kill its occupants, and put you in bankruptcy. GET RID OF IT IMMEDIATELY. The fireplaces in most mobile homes that came from the factory are not for heating but for looks.

How To Check For Problems?

If it exists, it is a problem

How To Fix Those Problems?

Get rid of it. Immediately.

How Difficult To Fix?

It does not matter. Get rid of it immediately.

Estimated Cost To Fix?

If you don't get rid of it -- so high it's hard to calculate.

Other Thoughts

What were they thinking of? And what are you thinking of it you leave it in there? The only one dumber than the person who put the aftermarket fireplace in is you if you don't remove it immediately.

Hud Seal

What Is This?

In 1976, the U.S. government passed construction standards for mobile homes and opened the "HUD Seal" era. When the HUD seal is on a mobile home, it means that it was built in conformance with this set of standards.

Types?

There is only one HUD seal. It is a metal plate, normally found in one of several locations: the hot water heater area, under the sink, in the door frame or on the body of the trailer.

Benefits & Drawbacks To Each?

Without a HUD seal, the home is of questionable construction standards.

The biggest disadvantage is that many municipalities will not allow a non-Hud seal home into their city. A HUD seal is extremely important, and it is absence may be an immediate deal killer for you.

How To Check For Problems?

Is there a seal or not? If there is paperwork, such as title, showing a manufacturer date after 1976, then it should have a seal, but you have to work at finding it.

Without a seal, and without paperwork showing the date of manufacturer, it is not a HUD code home.

How To Fix Those Problems?

If the home has no HUD seal, then there is nothing you can do about it except not buy it.

I would not, at this point in time, buy a non-HUD seal home.

How Difficult To Fix?

Impossible. Sorry.

Estimated Cost To Fix?

You can't buy a HUD seal.

Other Thoughts

This can be harder than a "Find Waldo" book.

Serial

What Is This?

This is the set of letters and numbers that documents the existence of the mobile home in a series of databases, and allows you to confirm such important information as title, liens, property taxes and the like.

Types?

There is only <u>one</u> serial number on a single wide (two for a double wide) and without it, it is hard to get the most important information on the home, and the information that could <u>really</u> come back to haunt you. Without the serial number, and the supporting documentation, you may find that you bought the home from someone who is not the real owner, does not have clear title or perhaps that the home has a big bank lien on it or unpaid property taxes. It may also keep you from moving the home, and definitely will make it hard or impossible to re-sell.

How To Check For Problems?

If you look in every conceivable place for the serial number (most importantly the frame), then the number may be gone.

In older homes, this is possible, especially pre 1976, since the serial number was often on a metal plate on the back of the home that could have fallen off or been removed when new siding was installed.

How To Fix Those Problems?

On newer homes a better bet is that it has been deliberately removed to hide a big issue, like an unpaid bank loan.

In some states, you can file paperwork to have a new serial number assigned to the home. However, this is far from a perfect process, and can take months to achieve.

Short of that, there is <u>nothing</u> you can do if the serial number is missing.

How Difficult To Fix?

In some states, with proper paperwork and a lot of time, you can get a new serial number.

Otherwise, it is impossible to fix.

Estimated Cost To Fix?

In some states, you can file for a replacement for about $150.00. In most cases, it is impossible regardless of cost.

Conclusion

Buying a used mobile home can be a profitable and positive experience, if you go about it in the right, informed way. There are plenty of pitfalls to avoid, and more than a few surprises that can pop up, but we believe that if you have read this book and keep the worksheet handy when evaluating homes for sale, you will have a great chance of doing a profitable job on your first try.

Always remember to minimize your liability and keep a tight handle on your renovation costs – these are the two factors that lead to ruin for most people. If you can perfect these skills, then you will be right up there with the pros right out of the chute.

Never be emotionally tied to a home for sale. Always be prepared to walk away from the deal if the numbers don't work. There is always another home to look at – normally just around the corner.

We hope that this book has put you on the right path and saves you thousands in mistakes.

Frank & Dave

CPSIA information can be obtained
at www.ICGtesting.com
Printed in the USA
BVHW030313231119
564632BV00002B/101/P